A NEW CENTURY IN RETROSPECT AND PROSPECT

James J. Van Patten

University Press of America
Lanham • New York • Oxford

Copyright © 2000 by
James J. Van Patten

University Press of America,® Inc.
4720 Boston Way
Lanham, Maryland 20706

12 Hid's Copse Rd.
Cumnor Hill, Oxford OX2 9JJ

Library of Congress Cataloging-in-Publication Data

Van Patten, James J.
A new century in retrospect and prospect / James J. Van Patten.
p.   cm.
Includes bibiographical references and index.
1.   Social prediction. 2. Economic forecasting. 3. Twenty-first century—
Forecasts. I. Title.
HM901.V363   2000   303.49—dc21   00—044329 CIP

ISBN 0-7618-1781-6 (cloth: alk. ppr.)
ISBN 0-7618-1782-4 (pbk: alk. ppr.)

⊖™ The paper used in this publication meets the minimum
requirements of American National Standard for Information
Sciences—Permanence of Paper for Printed Library Materials,
ANSI Z39.48—1984

Contents

Some Reflections on Media and the Future

Preface

The impetus for this book has been the undergraduate and graduate students with whom I have worked over the past thirty-seven years at
- Central Missouri State University, Warrensburg,
- University of Arkansas, Fayetteville,
- University of California at Los Angeles,
- University of Michigan at Ann Arbor,
- University of Florida, Gainesville,
- Peabody-Vanderbilt University at Nashville, and the
- University of Texas, Austin.

These students expressed their interest in and concern about a multidimensional society. They wondered about a more interconnected and interacting world; a world with interconnecting, interacting, interdependent, interdisciplinary study; a world with a global orientation toward problem solving.

Resources for this book included articles; and reports from print, broadcast and cable networks. I also utilized personal experiences shared with me by students, parents, colleagues, supervisors, administrators and people in private and corporate sectors of the workforce. These resources were utilized in classes to demonstrate the connections between the past with the future, and the connections between philosophy and emerging trends, issues and challenges.

It was always invigorating to learn about students' perceptions of the connections between theory and practice. Together we explored the present and projected changes that would affect each of us in both the academic and work-world. Some factors inhibiting positive changes for the future include:

1. an ever-changing corporate structure,
2. technology that required upgrading every year or sooner,
3. educational systems that were trying to respond to a multitude of often differing concerns by the public, parents, administrators, teachers, staff, and
4. an emerging leadership and government gridlock of confrontation, ill will, personal attacks, partisan bickering.

Some factors promoting positive changes for the future include:

1. volunteerism,
2. service learning, and
3. civic groups providing a sustained movement to improve our communities at the local level.

Analyzing the future through a variety of channels, influences and trends is challenging. Individuals are often reluctant to change and adapt to emerging paradigm shifts in the workplace or society as a whole. Those chief executive officers who do not adapt to changing markets will be fired or find their organizations deteriorating and forced to close. Yet, it is difficult to prepare for the future without the possibility of major errors. Ford Motor Company's Edsel and Coca Cola's "New Coke" are examples of misjudging the marketplace, even though both companies invested in detailed, extensive market polling analysis and advertising.

System breakdowns or unexpected events require strategic planning based on alternative scenarios for the future. Individuals and organizations need to engage in projecting three categories of trends: possible, preferable and probable. Why don't organizations and businesses make accurate projections? Far too often organizations fail to encourage the cooperation and teamwork necessary, and instead, they get entangled in a web of turf defense. Horizontal communication networks can break down boundary, "in the box" thinking and can empower individuals to engage in creative, innovative and visionary responses which could be beneficial to a positive quality organizational climate.

Synergy is created when individuals feel they are stakeholders in their workplaces. Whether in corporate, governmental or educational institutions, addressing entropy (all living systems run down) through a variety of initiatives is essential.

Ways to Combat Entropy and Atrophy
• reorganization
• restructuring
• hiring new people
• providing opportunities for employees to gain experience in a wide variety of jobs within the organization

These are early systemic responses to atrophy, complacency, poor morale, and turf defense. These initiatives toward change need not be threatening to senior employees, especially if opportunities are provided to include everyone in the process of change. Senior employees bring their knowledge, experience, and expertise which can be tapped to avoid costly errors in change processes. On the other hand, upper-level managers often find it difficult to dismiss senior employees who are nonproductive, out of touch, or embittered. The responsibility for firing disgruntled employees who are "stuck in the way things used to be" is often passed down the management line.

Historically, some large corporation managers shifted unproductive, inefficient workers to other jobs in which they could perform well and become assets again. IBM was often referred to in the past as a corporation that always found a job within the organization that employees could perform well. The days of accommodating problem or "stale" employees appear to be extinct as success in global competition requires downsizing and creates increased competition throughout the workforce.

Corporations, universities, colleges, public schools and local, state, regional, national organizations—all groups continually scan the future. Scanning the environmental and analyzing an organization's strengths and weaknesses, future prospects, and realistic choices is a useful tool for anticipating problems and creating innovations. For example, universities are currently faced with changes in delivery systems for an emerging marketplace of geographically separated and other non-traditional students. New and rapidly changing technology and an increasing demand for accountability challenge old assumptions.

Distance learning systems were developed to provide for placebound students. Placebound students have full time jobs, families, and are unable to fit their schedules into traditional place and time constraints. University of Phoenix, (found in Phoenix, Arizona and other U.S. cities) is a non-traditional higher education institution with some 45,000 students. The University of Phoenix has no athletic teams, dorms, or traditional trappings or frills. Faculty are often part-time and untenured, but they are required to have extensive experience in the fields in which they teach. The clientele comprises mostly adult, non-traditional students. Access to learning resources is through computers (e-mail, listservs, news groups, and the World Wide Web) and materials provided by instructors. Nova Southeastern University Ft. Lauderdale, Florida is another innovative model that provides opportunities for full time jobholders to earn a degree through a flexible delivery program. Both institutions are accredited by the associations in their areas. Accreditation provides important benchmarking to assure quality of courses and degree programs consistent with the best national and international guidelines in the various academic areas. Accreditation gives institutions a quality label for perspective students and employers of their students.

Traditional research universities are responding to new learning models by offering evening, Saturday and distance learning classes. These non-traditional, non-residential, courses and degree programs are the fastest growing delivery systems in the country. With knowledge doubling every 20 months or less, flexibility, mobility, and change will continue to be a trend. Our grandparents performed a lifetime of work for a single organization. People today must prepare for a work life with three or more career changes. So we can predict recycling and retraining for adults and lifelong education will be a necessity in the future. Preparing a future filled with possibilities and opportunities is vital in the 21st century.

The predictions of respected journalists, futurists, academics, and administrators, have occasionally been proven wrong. Following are a few historical examples of firm convictions that were proven erroneous (Cerf and Navasky, 1998).

> **Democracy's future:**
>
> If...there is any conclusion in politics on which we can securely rely, both from history, and from the laws which govern human action, it is this, *that universal suffrage and freedom never were and never can be co-existent.*
>
> John Augustine Smith
> (Professor of Moral and Political Philosophy and
> President of the College of William and Mary, 1817.)
>
> What do we want with this vast, useless area (the West)? This region of savages and wild beasts, of deserts, of shifting sands and whirlwinds of dust, of cactus and prairie dogs? To what use could we ever hope to put these great deserts, or those endless mountain ranges, impenetrable and covered to their very base with eternal snow? What can we ever hope to do with the Western coast?
>
> Daniel Webster (U.S. Senator from Massachusetts),
> Denouncing a Congressional bill to establish a mail route
> From Missouri to the West Coast, 1829.
>
> Atmospheric nuclear tests do not seriously endanger either present or future generations.

There will be missteps, erroneous future projections, and many adjustments as organizations modify, change, and reformulate future plans to maintain their viability.

During the writing of this book, governmental gridlock, partisanship, hate language, intolerance, dogmatism, and acts of violence, were societal issues that required legal recourse and other coping mechanisms. Men and women of goodwill were called upon to improve their individual communities through local action, regardless of national stalemate on certain issues.

As we analyze our future from past experiences, it is clear that a balance between divergent forces always occurs. Whether Marx's theory of conflict of classes or Aristotle's Golden Mean or modern systems theory, paradigm shifts lead to a new search for balance and a new language of compromise and promise. If this work challenges readers to contemplate opportunities and prepare for challenges in a new century, it will have fulfilled its purpose. Any polemical writing within the text can be attributed to the author's own workplace and life experiences. However, all of us are facing a new century. The Internet and other computer technology may influence society for good or evil. No one knows exactly how technology will shape the future. Living during a transition to a new century always stimulates reflection on the past and predictions for the future.

Most individuals will continue to look forward to an exciting new venture in our new 21st century. A few groups such as the Heaven's Gate sect committed collective suicide to coincide with the approach of the comet Hale-Bopp while others engaged in bizarre activities to usher in a new era. All their fears have proven to be unfounded. The Y2K concerns illustrated how widely publicized threats led to excessive action and reaction. Living at the early years of a new century always stimulates reflection on the past and predictions of the future.

This book is designed to address alternative issues and challenges for a new millenium. At the turn of the 20th century there was a paradigm shift from an agrarian to an industrial society. At the turn of the 21st century, we face a paradigm shift from industrial to a post-industrial global information superhighway which will expand and extend our knowledge access and dissemination possibilities. The Internet is an information highway without boundaries that ameliorate differences in ethnicity, culture, nationality, gender, age and racial identities. It is possible that the Internet will eventually break the foundation of authoritarian, totalitarian, and dictatorial governments leading to more open societies. We need to provide young people with the skills to evaluate the quality of information available on the Internet. As the tragic violence at Columbine High School in Littleton, Colorado demonstrated, there is a deviant and violent subculture on the Internet that encourages and promotes hate and destruction. While freedom to access information is essential in a free, pluralistic, interdependent world; we need to provide the knowledge individuals need to be able to sift the good from the bad, and make responsible choices as they use the Internet or whatever the next wave of technology will be.

Linda Sharp McElhiney's editorial guidance was invaluable in this project. Robert Sherman, University of Florida, Gainesville; Timothy J. Bergen, Interim Associate Dean, University of South Carolina; Dean Jim R. Bowman, Central Missouri State University, Warrensburg, Missouri; James T. Bolding, Emeritus, Martin W. Schoppmeyer, Emeritus, Hugh Mills, Emeritus, Buddy Lyle and Rhonda Harvey, Adult/Vocational Education, Tommie Van Asten, University of

Arkansas, Fayetteville reviewed the manuscript and provided advice and direction for the undertaking. Educational administrators, Jerry Siegrist, Valdosta State University, Valdosta, Georgia; Ann Witcher, University of Central Arkansas, Conway; Fred Kierstead, futurist University of Houston, Clearlake, Texas; John Pulliam, University of Montana, Missoula, Emeritus Dean; Roderick McDavis, former Dean of Education, University of Florida, Gainesville; Dean Charles Stegman, Dean of Education, and Chris Lucas, Department Chair of Educational Leadership, University of Arkansas provided encouragement and inspiration for this book. Each has been in higher education institutions for six to over thirty years and has made major contributions in the areas of their expertise. Special appreciation must go to Brandi Holt, Ed.D., a former graduate assistant now with Wal Mart, McNeel Gordon, graduate assistant, Florida Atlantic University, Liz Lewis, an outstanding secretary and computer expert who has graciously formatted this manuscript for publication, and Anita Van Patten whose repeated proofreading and editorial advice was essential to this project's completion.

James J. Van Patten, Ph.D.

A New Century in Retrospect and Prospect

James J. Van Patten
University of Arkansas Fayetteville

....History is shaped as much by intangibles as hard facts. The biggest changes of the twentieth century were not foreseen by the experts. They had no way of anticipating the tides of political change that were to sweep over the world. They had no way of knowing where or how human hopes or fears would be suddenly created into vast sources of energy that would transform political, economic, and social institutions.

Norman Cousins, 1974

Technical Views

Our world faces a paradigm shift in a historical transitional period of significant change. Such change always invokes resistance as old myths are challenged and new visions are created by human and moral energy. As we move into an electronic village in our workplaces, homes and schools, we can involve all participants in a democratic process. Resistance to change, however difficult, will give way as the superinformation highway with e-commerce leads the way into a new-world order. In some organizations a culture of traditional leadership mindset will be disruptive to progress in multifaceted, multi-dimensional communication requiring a world interdependence paradigm shift, so essential for our new century. Politics will be the challenge as it may delay, retard, or limit needed funding for a new communication generation. The information age with knowledge overloads will require a sense of balance in order to respect the privacy rights of citizens, their human dignity, and their self-esteem. Finding a role for spirituality in a machine-oriented age is essential to provide for humane and human values in a technological age.

Reaffirming a commitment to social and economic justice will provide a process of continual renewal for individuals and society. This renewal will require an open, welcoming sense of community—cultural, intellectual, social resources—to provide an underpinning of an open, pluralistic society. These values will shape the order, dignity, worth, and respect for future generations.

If one were to look back at our present transitional period from 100 years in the future, it might appear as if all knowledge systems were in a state of perpetual flux, challenging each other for dominance. What in our present might seem like a tangled web of chaos with affirmation and negation challenging each other, from the distance would reflect the glory of emancipation from a limited, boundary oriented world, to an unlimited boundless world of infinite possibilities for the betterment of humankind. Critics and doomsayers would view such a vision as a hopeless romantic, idealistic vision only for dreamers. Futurists might refer to the magnitude of challenges in our age as opportunities for recreating a more humane social order.

It is in the nature of humans to plan for the future. We look ahead to tomorrow, to plan for financial security, for raising families, for preparing ourselves and our offspring for better jobs through education at all levels, K-12, Community Colleges, Universities. Each of us has hopes, visions, dreams of personal fulfillment and professional growth.

This book provides a compilation of alternative scenarios by futurists together with an examination of current initiatives in business, industry, government, and education that will alter our workforce, our leisure time, our relationships with one another and the totality of our lives. No single factor can be examined in isolation from the totality of forces, trends, and influences which are continually in a state of interaction, flux, and the ebb and flow of change which affect the future.

Heilbroner: The Future as History

....We need an attitude which accepts the outlook of the historic future without succumbing to false hopes or to an equally false despair; a point of view which sees in the juggernaut of history's forces both the means by which progress painfully made in the past may be trampled underfoot, and the means by which a broader and stronger base for progress in the future may be brought into being.

Robert L. Heilbroner, *The Future as History*

Heilbroner sought an understanding of the dynamic of history's forces in preparing the way for eventual progress. Only from such a sense of historic understanding can come the strength to pass through the gauntlet with integrity of mind and spirit. Heilbroner continued by noting that:

We cannot help living in history....If we are to meet, endure, and transcend the trials and defeats of the future—for trials and defeats there are certain to be—it can only be from a point of view which, seeing the future as part of the sweep of history, enables us to establish our place in that immense procession in which it is incorporated whatever hope humankind can have (p.208-209).

Heilbroner foresaw that no matter what its difficulties, the painful evolution beyond present-day capitalism is indispensable if those nations which have gained the benefits of material wealth are now to cope rationally with its administration.

Our Puritan forefathers came to the New World to develop and maintain an ideal society. Puritans founded Harvard in 1636, created the Olde Deluder Satan Act in 1642 to provide for a common school whenever there were 50 families in a community and a companion act in 1647 to provide a tutor for boys with talent whenever a community grew to 100 families. True from our vantage point the Puritan Society became a community of pinched narrow-minded fanatics, but each of us is a prisoner of the age in which we live. The Puritans over time gave us the Congregational Church, a lively sense of philosophical debate about individuals' relations to the larger cosmos, a keen sense of questioning the control, financing, goals and consequences of education. They, as we, sought to define what is ultimately worth knowing. The town meeting, community participation in local issues, and initial steps in the formation of democratic theory and practice were legacies of the Puritans. Dissenters who were banished from the Old Massachusetts Bay Colony, created new communities that provided opportunities for pluralism in the new society. As these new communities grew, so did pluralism in the composition of our society. Through a series of wars, the fight for independence from England became fulfilled with the adoption and implementation of the Constitution in 1789. Each step along the way was built on compromise and visions of a future of a United States. The bill of rights, ratified in 1791, represented efforts to clarify individual and state rights not included in the original Constitution. The first amendment provided for freedom of speech, religion, the press, the right to assemble peaceably, and to petition the government for redress of grievances. Jefferson's Louisiana Purchase was an impetus to Westward Expansion. Jefferson's meritocracy and Jacksonian egalitarianism, a series of wars—the Revolutionary War, War of 1812, Mexican War, The Civil War, the Spanish American War, World War I and II, the Korean, the Vietnam War, and the Gulf War—unified and influenced the future shape of American society. Several of the wars were fought to protect and maintain global markets, essential for an overproducing nation. Self-searching during and after the Vietnamese War led to questioning national policy. There was a brief period of a national boost of confidence after the Gulf War. In recent years there have been continued efforts to find diplomatic solutions to conflicts although threats of military strikes to enforce United Nations policies are retained as an option. Recent unilateral bombing of Iraq without full prior United Nations concurrence may lead to unforeseen multiplier effects, although any prediction about foreign trouble spots are subject to caution. The world community through the United Nations continues to stress the urgency of seeking peaceful solutions to local and regional conflicts. United States Congress and governmental leaders continue to debate their role as world policeman in the global trouble spots.

Progress toward a common set of values has been variable with periods of advance in technology, economic and social justice, and expansion of social consciousness, together with a continuance of bias, intolerance, prejudice as witness treatment of Native Americans, Women, the elderly, African Americans, Hispanics, Asian Americans and other minority groups. A growing middle class with an ever-expanding governmental support network for individuals at risk provided the nation with social and economic stability. Our national history gives us an evolutionary view of change and stability over time. In a special Golden Anniversary issue of *The Saturday Review World* of August 24, 1974, a number of world leaders were asked to place themselves in 2024 and look back. McGeorge Bundy, President of Ford Foundation, a former Harvard Dean and professor of government before becoming special assistant for national security affairs for Presidents Kennedy and Johnson reviewed the cost to the French and Germans, the Japanese and Americans, and the Israelis and the Arabs, of learning to be friends. Bundy examined the challenge of working to end hunger and nuclear danger at home and abroad, while seeking to understand from a distant future the challenge of underemployment and inflation. Historical watersheds provide us with a roadmap to a more humane future.

As we explore the future, building blocks will be formed as the basis for our visions. These building blocks are the doors through which each of us can envision the challenges and opportunities of the future. Thinking globally and acting locally, individuals can challenge forces of resistance.

Future Scenarios

It is difficult to predict or engage in forecasting the future. Scenario building and trend extrapolation have been helpful in envisioning trends, but there are always system breaks (unexpected events, happenings, occurrences) that need to be taken into account when writing about possible, preferable and probable futures. Ridenour (1998), president of the National Center for Public Policy identified a few Worldwatch Institute predictions gone awry. In 1987, the environmentalist institute predicted an oil shortage would cause a major energy crisis in five years. Currently due in part to new technology to find oil, the industry is producing more oil than it can sell and the price has dropped from $21 a barrel in 1981 to under $5 in 1998. The Worldwide Institute predicted in 1985 that U.S., British and Mexican oil reserves would be depleted within fifteen years and Middle Eastern producers would have a monopoly on oil. Worldwatch viewed wind and solar energy as the energy sources of the future in 1985. The prediction may still come true in the far distant future, but to date such energy sources have provided minimal energy for the nation's needs. In 1987, Worldwatch's Christopher Flavin reported that the Chernobyl nuclear accident marked the beginning of the end for such power sources, while in 1987 there were 437 operating nuclear power plants, with nearly everyone in the United States receiving at least some electricity from nuclear power. These environmentalist's predictions, if not currently accurate, provide food for thought for the future. In rebuttal, Christopher Flavin and Seth Dunn (1998) Vice President and Research Associate, at Worldwide Institute reported that remaining oil sources are so limited that world production will peak in 15-20 years and that wind and solar power are growing at rates of between 16 and 25 percent a year. In analyzing futurist's predictions it is important to examine their overt and covert agendas.

Molitor, Christie Whitman, John Kerry and a Newsweek team of Pat Wingert, Karen Springen, Elizabeth Angell and Michael Meyer shared some current trends that are particularly timely as we move closer to a new millennium. Their identified trends are changing our lifestyles, workplaces, and visions of tomorrow.

Molitor (1998) spent five years compiling the *Encyclopedia of the Future*. Some of his predictions include:

Communications

- Increased investments in improving information superhighways.
- Continued business investments in computer technologies. Since 1991 business has spent more money on computer and communications hardware than for factories, buildings and other durables.
- Information technologies are allowing increasing numbers of people to work at home. The number may reach over 60 million in 1998.
- Telecommuting and advances in videoconferencing will largely replace face to face business settings by 2020.

Medical Breakthroughs

- Diagnostics will advance rapidly in the next 50 years. Credit card sized diagnostic plates consisting of up to a million or more microcell probes—arrays of miniature test tubes—to detect dysfunctions will be read and analyzed by computers in minutes.
- Wearable computerized health monitors will provide timely information on diet, exercise and stress reduction initiatives.
- Cloning technologies will be developed for prolonging life.

Household Size

- Households are getting smaller with more singles and mingles (housemates and cohabiting couples).
- Family units will wane and not be the primary social unit in the future. Patriarchal dominance will atrophy as women achieve fully equal rights.

Reardon and Obejas (1999) reported that family life in America at the dawn of the new millennium is immensely more complex than it was in the 1950s. Back then, the nuclear family was the dominant family form in the United States. Some experts estimate that 39% of all American women and 30% of all children are likely to spend time in a stepfamily. Reardon and Obejas continued by noting that some 9 million American families with children under 18 are headed by a single parent, an increase of nearly 200 percent since 1970.

How We Live and How We Used to Live

Married couples still account for more than half of the 102.5 million households in the U.S. or some 53 percent of the total in 1998.

1970	Demographics	1998
40%	Traditional Family-married couples with children under 18 including step families with young children	25%
30%	Married Couples/No Young Children	28%
12%	Women Living Alone, Elderly Widows, Young Adults	15%
6%	Men Living Alone, Young or Middle Aged, Elderly	11%
5%	Single Mothers and Young Children	8%
4%	Single Mother/No Young Children	5%
2%	Roommates, gay couples, unmarried heterosexual couples	5%
1%	Single Father and Young Children	2%
1%	Single Father/No Young Children, Grandfathers Included	2%
(Source: Chicago Tribune Analysis of Data from U.S. Census Bureau. Sunday March 21, 1999: Section 13, 5).		

Aging

- Society will grow older; the sixty-five and older population may represent 27% of the population by 2050. Thau and Heflin (1997) find that the U.S. population over age 70 is expected to double by 2030. The cost of supporting this population may lead to increased tension between retired baby boomers and a middle-aged Generation X'ers. There are proposals to increase the social security retirement age to keep the security system viable. Senior citizens wield political power through the ballot while younger citizens often do not vote. They are either too busy working, raising a family or lack interest in the political process. Thau and Heflin note that some individuals believe the situation may not be as serious as some believe. Older Americans often save enough during their working years to be able to meet health care costs throughout their later years. In addition, many seniors work out of a desire to continue to contribute to society or to remain active in their lives. Often seniors serve as volunteers to meet needs of various populations at risk.

Epstein (1998) finds estimates of the world population in 2100 at between 9.1 billion with a medium estimate of 11.1 billion. These estimates assume life expectancies of 82.5 years for males and 87.5 years for females in mid-century. Epstein notes a trend toward decreased family size in Latin America, and Asia. Population growth remains high in Africa, the Caribbean and the South Asian subcontinent. Estimating population trends remains a problematical study regardless of sophisticated research methodologies. A variety of factors including have and have not nations, upward economic mobility, women entering and staying in the workforce in increasing numbers, women holding leadership positions in corporations, industry, educational institutions, affect population trends. In an effort to reduce population growth, one-child families are official policy in The People's Republic of China, but in Western nations the expense of child rearing and a desire to continue working by women of childbearing age, leads to ever-smaller families. Although estimates vary, Western Nations generally average 2 children per woman in her childbearing years.

Molitor continued by noting that:

- The trend toward early retirement will be reversed, rising to 70 in 2025. More age-centered political controversies will arise especially over government spending as programs for the elderly may increase from one-third of federal spending to one-half by 2010.
- Some enterprises will thrive on senior citizens. New motor vehicle operating systems will be designed for people with reduced dexterity and publishers will produce books with large type for those with reduced vision.
- There will be more design features in homes and cars to accommodate the physically challenged population.

Business and the Economy

- Business may be increasingly oriented to leisure, recreation, tourism and hospitality sectors.
- Global competition will spur major U.S. manufacturers to shift employment to low-wage areas and minimize costly regulatory controls.
- Companies will turn increasingly to outsourcing capital-intensive functions.
- Electronic commerce will take over more and more retail and wholesale commerce.
- Electronic shopping and home delivery will play a larger role in the future.

Personal Finance

- Stockholding is becoming democratized. Some 41% of U.S. households have become stockholders.
- Personal debt is growing, putting a damper on consumer spending and savings. Mortgages and home-equity loan payments totaled $4.22 trillion in 1993, and installment payments on credit cards reached $1.17 trillion in 1996. By mid-1997, service payments on consumer debt approached 11.5% of disposable income, outpacing spending on food.

- The number of personal bankruptcies climbed to 1.3 million in the United States in 1997 and will exceed 1.5 million by 2000.
- Education costs at private schools more than doubled in twenty years in the United States from $25,514 in 1974 to $64,410 in 1994 and are likely to double again by 2014.

Transportation

- The world's fleet of cars will continue to grow from 625 million motor vehicles to 1 billion by 2025.
- Traffic jams in the United States consumed an estimated 1.6 billion lost work hours in 1989 and will consume 8.1 billion work hours by 1005. During 1997, traffic gridlock cost $51 billion in lost wages and things will get worse as motor vehicle ownership escalates.
- Vehicles and drivers will increase from 25% to 35% in 2010.
- Automated highways and automated chauffeuring on high-density roadways will reduce congestion, allowing 10 times as many vehicles in computer-controlled chains to travel in a lane.
- Motor vehicle emission taxes will be imposed by 2013 to curb urban pollution.
- Superfast rail systems approaching speeds of 200 mph will collapse distances for suburban areas.

Molitor also noted that the world's fund of information is doubling every two to two and one-half years. Scientific information doubles every five years, and scientific knowledge doubles every ten years. Literature doubles every 10-15 years; scientific articles double every four to five years.

By the time a child born today finishes college knowledge may have quadrupled; by the time that child reaches age 50, knowledge will have grown 32 fold. As much as 97% of the world's knowledge will be accumulated over one person's lifetime. Continuing education becomes a fixed feature of infotech (Molitor, 1998).

Salzman and Matathia (1998) identified possible lifestyles for a new millennium. Included in their forecasts are:

- Company towns with subsidized apartments, houses, condos wired to the workplace with larger corporations building campuses, completed with onsite child, and elder care, health facilities and personal services concierges.
- Granny minders with in-home infrared detectors that monitor an individual's daily routines to allow elderly persons to live independently longer. An absence of activity, such as not opening the refrigerator during the day will trigger an automatic distress call to a caregiver.
- Divorce insurance.
- Nannycams hidden inside teddy bears and other security measures will give parents virtual access to their children at daycare at all times. Latchkey kids will have camera surveillance systems so parents can view their children's activities when they are unsupervised.
- Enforced parental responsibility with parents paying the price for their children's illegal activities. Parents may have insurance policies to protect them from financial responsibilities for their children's illegal activities.

Technology

Technological skills have become so important in our society, that parents seek to have their babies become familiar with the information age. Chmielewski (1998) reported that parents have their six to sixteen month-old babies get a feel for CD-ROM games like JumpStart Baby and place computer mice in their offspring's hands so they can be prepared for computers even before toddlers are taught to handle a spoon or fork. Although educators debate the benefits of early computer experience, sales of children's software have doubled in the past year from $9.7 million in the first quarter of 1997 to $17.9 million in 1998 (Chmielewski: 3F).

Tyson (1998) reinforces parental concerns about having their children learn about computers at an ever-younger age. Tyson reports 1996 online shopping revenues have surged 10-fold to $7 billion with a projection of $41 billion in sales by 2002. He reported that Internet commerce will reshape the global economy as commerce sales or online trade in goods and services among businesses and between business and consumers will reach as high as $3.2 trillion in 2003 or 5% of all global sales. Tyson concluded by reporting that digital traffic doubles every 100 days with companies like Amazon.com increasing sales in 1997 by over 825 percent from the year earlier.

The proposed AOL/Netscape merger, if approved, will advance e-commerce, according to Sandberg (1998) may lead to a period of TV set-top boxes, video-phones and wireless devices tapping the power of the Internet. E-commerce, cybershopping, is one of the fastest growing phenomena of our time. Levy (1998) noted that cybershopping, while easier if technology is working correctly, often can become a harrowing experience. After spending an hour or more Internet shopping the system may freeze, leaving the shopper in the lurch. President Clinton has directed the Commerce Department and FTC to step up cyberfraud enforcement due to an increased number of buyers who report being ripped off by unethical sellers, according to Levy. The Internet is still in the process of developing, still in its infancy, and in the years ahead, it will be more closely monitored, become more reliable and cheaper for the general public.

The Clinton and Gore administrations have been committed to finding ways to speed the process of having the nation's schools networked to the Internet. Meanwhile there will be continued efforts in our schools to have pupils become Internet literate. Pupils will be protected from pornography, and other unethical information by cyberpatrol management. They will be taught to access quality information for their research and schoolwork and to ignore misleading, unreliable, and false information. Students can access the Library of Congress, and other university library cites throughout the country to receive quality information.

Collie (1998) reported on kids power in the modern market. Collie found kids are more knowledgeable about technology and about resource sites availability on the Internet. Kids are less fearful of using technology and often teach others how to use the machines. Technology is influencing how children conceptualize shapes, patterns, relationships, and meaning. Nearing the 21st century, electronics plays an ever larger role in the lives of youth. Collie noted that the percentage of children 9-17 with electronics in their bedroom included:

Television	59%
Cable/Satellite	55%
Telephone	42%
Stereo	42%
Computer	40%
VCR	39%
Video Game System	36%
Portable CD Player	21%

School children often carry cellular phones and beepers communicating with peers, parents and others more frequently. Using computers for games is an increasing passion for youngsters as well as improving their physical motor skills.

Talbott (1995) examined the complexity of human-machine interaction in his book *The Future Does Not Compute:*

- The computer took shape in the human mind before it was realized in the world.
- What we embed in the computer is the inert and empty shadow, or abstract reflection, of the past operation of our own intelligence.
- The computer gains a certain autonomy—runs by itself—on the strength of its embedded reflection of human intelligence. We are thus confronted from the world by the active powers of our own, most mechanistic mental functioning.
- Having reconceived my own interior as computation, and having them embedded a reflection of this interior in the computer, I compulsively seek fulfillment—the completion of myself—through the interface.

- Man is he who knows and transforms himself—and the world—from within. He is the future speaking (Talbott: 360, 383).

A caveat should be noted about future projections, predictions, and prophecies. As we approach a new century, our technological information age with its unlimited possibility for improvement in living standards, economic and societal advances, there is a need for improving the dependability of our technology. Those of us who spend an increasing amount of our work life on computers, networking with others, accessing information on a variety of search engines, often face frustration, and alienation as our systems accuse us of committing illegal operations, screens blank out, viruses contaminate our manuscripts, and carefully gathered and written information is obliterated. Data destruction, incompatible computer systems, require standby troubleshooters who are often so overloaded with requests for assistance that response times for help are unbearable. Technical support requires sitting in front of your computer with all applicable serial numbers while wading through a maze of menus often taking excessively long periods to talk to a human. Meanwhile with music playing in the background, announcements of new products from time to time with an occasional "please do not hang up. Your call is important to us. You will lose your cue in line should you hang up and have to start from scratch again. Thank you for continuing to hold. Most of our employees are at lunch now but will be back shortly". Often a response is "Thank you for calling our technical support system. Unfortunately phone lines are overloaded, and you have lost your place in line. Please push one if you would like to be connected again to technical support." Not infrequently a customer finally gets a response requesting a credit card number for billing. Unfortunately due to an unexpected additional lengthy wait, the customer must hang up the phone to return to work. The consequence is it may take several months to a year to remove the invoiced amount from the credit card bill.

E-mail Internet systems are often undependable making it difficult to keep up with demands for increased production. When computers and access systems are working well, workers are often inundated with unwanted and inaccurate information. Some e-mail messages are so comprehensive computers need to be upgraded to handle them.

Fine (1998) reported that Internet users often become shocked and frightened by hate messages. An Internet user clicked on the Web site of a hate group. Fine noted that the Pennsylvania attorney general's office shut down a white-supremacist web site in October 1998. The site spewing forth messages of vitriolic hate, creates an issue of the struggle to weigh free speech on the Internet against possible harm. Other anti-abortion, racist, and protest groups spew forth their anti-civilized, inhumane, and uncivil ideologies. Fine noted that Barry Steinhardt, President of the Electronic Frontier Foundation believes the free-speech battles of the 21st century will be fought in cyberspace.

Telephone message menus are so detailed, it often takes a great deal of time to access accurate information. Often individuals cannot access the information they need. Governmental agencies information systems of IRS, Immigration Service, Social Security are extremely difficult to access. Some individuals find it takes weeks to get needed information and not infrequently drive to distant Immigration Offices where on-site contacts provide limited services. Another telephone challenge is to reach computer technicians from Microsoft/ Hewlett-Packard or other major computer and technology companies. Prior to answering requests for help on solving computer problems, credit card identification is required to assure up-front payment for information that may not solve problems. Occasionally customers have to wait so long for service, they must to hang up to fulfill job commitments. Such a situation leads to being billed for services not received and a hassle to get the bill in dispute off the credit card statements.

Another caveat for commerce on the Internet is misinformation or lack of information for customers. As Kirchner (1999) pointed out it is essential to give customers accurate information as to editorial content and advertising. Amazon.com, a pioneering bookseller, recently acknowledged that some of its books that received its buying recommendations, made the list due to large payments from publishers. Kirchner continued by noting that if readers and viewers can't trust editorial content, they may not continue to purchase advertised materials. The Internet commerce is in the process of developing and it may be essential in the future to monitor the ethics of advertisers.

Wildstrom (1998) found that home computers are too complex and simpler appliances are on the way. He reported that over time complex computers systems will be replaced by an assortment of devices, specialized to perform a specific task—Palm Pilot to manage address books and calendars, CrossPad digital clipboards to load handwritten information into a computer, printers that can use memory cards from digital cameras to print pictures directly, and networks to connect appliances within and outside the home. Another emerging simplified device on the market accesses information for Web Browsing, word processing, E-mail, financial management and other uses through television screens using a computer keyboard and network box.

New frontiers in technology are computer modeling to forecast marketing trends, to design automobiles and for a multitude of other purposes. Often focus groups are utilized as background information sources for computer extrapolation. Such extrapolation provides a base for computer market research. Complexity theory explains the multidimensional powers of computer projections. Virtual reality serves as a means of modeling future life styles. Simulation models, however sophisticated, are subject to system breaks. Russian economic collapse, Coca Cola's failure of its new soft drink, the Ford Edsel, illustrate the dangers of overemphasis on survey research however well designed, and implemented. Regardless of significant failures, computer complexity, modeling, virtual reality and artificial intelligence will be the wave of the future as refinement, correction, modification, and increased reliability improve creativity, forecasts and new product development.

Combs (1998) reported on a Second International Symposium on Wearable Computers. Forecasts include conclusions that by 2020 individuals will be able to recite a list of needed groceries into a microphone built into her lenses. Inside the store, the woman's identification ring will broadcast her buying habits to the store computer, which will beam discount prices to the monitor in her eyeglasses. With computer advances doubling every 18 months, visions of computers tiny enough to sew into everyday clothing, may become a reality. She concluded by describing a pair of ordinary-looking, black rimmed glasses that was on display with a built in monitor. The translucent display, the width of a pencil eraser, sat in the middle of one eyeglass lens. A wearer could see the image of a monitor that appeared to be 3 feet away, a quarter of the size of a normal screen, but with a translucent monitor did not block a wearer's view.

The rapidity and extension of our technological age is influencing every aspect of our society.

End of a revolution?

In 1971 zealous Intel chip designers figured out a way to pack 2,300 transistors onto a thumbnail-size sliver of silicon to make the first microprocessor. The PC revolution was born. For the next 20 years the number of transistors doubled every 24 months, or about 40% a year, in keeping with Moore's Law. That's a 520-fold increase; processing speed rose 305-fold.

But in the 1990s the law began to peter out. Since 1993 the transistor count has risen at a pace of only 21% a year. Pentium III boasts 9.5 million transistors—but that is up only 27% in two years.

It matters not: Intel chips have far outpaced the ability of software to use all that power. Most of today's uses, such as Microsoft Word and Excel spreadsheets, are easily handled by the first, now-primitive Pentiums of six years ago.

Only the most advanced uses—voice recognition, video, game-playing on the Web—need more power. Yet the Pentium III crunches so fast that even cable modems have a hard time keeping up. Better software and wider bandwidth may help, but the trendline is clear. This revolution is starting to sputter.
    –BRETT NELSON

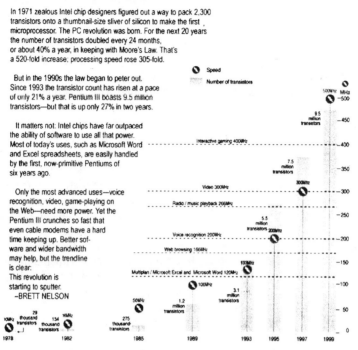

Source: Intel; Forrester Research; Microsoft; Dragon Systems. (Forbes May 3rd 1999)

As Wildstrom (1998) noted, future uses of technology will be simpler, more reliable, and efficient. It would be truly wonderful if individuals could write a letter or search the Web without being constantly warned about committing an illegal operation that could wipe out all data. University faculty often have to console students who have had their computers wipe out complete dissertations even though students saved the data frequently. Students often find out the hard way, that keeping hard copies of rough drafts and raw data is essential.

Lohr and Markoff (1998) reported that once networks are extremely fast there will be centralized intelligence, accessible through fast computer networks. They found one group of technologists find a post-PC era due to the creation of intelligent networks, linked by powerful hub computers, feeding data to millions of information appliances such as cell phones, hand-held and other devices, each with a built in microchip to receive remote instructions. Other technologists see the computer as continuing to be a major player but in a smaller, cheaper, more mobile, and easier to use form—a post-PC plus era. IBM has set up a pervasive computing unit to prepare for a post-PC world, concluding after a year-long study that future trends will involve near term benefits for conveniences such as calling a toll free number while away from a home base, leaving voice-mail instructions to receive specific e-mail messages for reading on the display screen of a cell phone (Lohr and Markoff: C3).

Yaukey (1999) reported that there is a trend toward miniaturization of everything. MEMS representing a marriage of supersmall computer chips with tiny sensors, probes, lasers and actuators will underpin the next generation of electronics, communications and medical devices while creating entirely new technology. MEMS is a still-nascent field called nanotechnology in which scientists envision turning building blocks of matter itself (individual atoms and molecules) into microscopic machines. Yaukey concludes that although history is a graveyard of futuristic visions that fell flat, MEMS may provide scientists with the ability to imbue simple materials with intelligence. These devices can think like a computer chip, and act by releasing chemicals or drugs, by readjusting themselves to dance with the shaking of an earthquake or by glowing to alert mechanics to an otherwise invisible crack in an airplane strut or a bridge girder. The future of technology appears to include infinite possibilities for expanding our knowledge and its applications to improvement in communication, health care, and quality of life in a new era.

Digital Epochs

From the precursors of the mainframe computer to the current crop of hand-held computerized devices, each new digital era has meant an exponential increase in the number of computing machines.

1940's	1950's	1960's	1970's	80's 90's	2000's
Pre-Mainframe	Mainframe	Minicomputer	Personal Computer		Post-PC.
Early Example	Eniac	IBM 701	Digital Equip	PDP 1 MITS Altair	Post-PC
Impact	Computation exceeding the capabilities of mechanical calculators.	Vast new number crunching powers for the elite	Mainframe at a size and cost within reach of many companies	Minicomputer capabilities at a size and cost within the reach of individuals	Low cost products tailored to specific uses
Number of Machines	One	Thousands	Hundreds of Thousands	Hundreds of Millions	Billions
Lohr and Markoff, *New York Times*, December 28, 1998: C 1.					

The future of technology is fraught with challenges that need to be met before possibilities become working realities.

Slambrouck (1998) interviewed Manuel Castells, an ex-Marxist and futurist. Castells viewed the basic structure of society as far-flung networks, not the individual companies, governments and institutions defined in the 19th century power grid. Castells finds society, aided by needed digital technology, is rapidly reorganizing itself around networks. These networks are a kind of infinitely adaptable organisms that have no center, unlike traditional governments, and no geographic boundaries. Castells finds networks as the primary means by which society is organized. Internet communications will provide for communities of interest which can change rapidly. Culture will be, according to Castells, defined less and less by direct experiences because our life, our work, our experience will be in the virtual world. Technology will change our lives, expand our horizons, eliminate boundaries and divisions, but the value of technology in practice depends on how people use this power to improve people's quality of life throughout the world.

Futurists live in a political world. Politicians have a stake in analyzing alternative scenarios for the future and there is a *Congressional Clearing House for the Future* that compiles information about trends and issues for a new millennium. Following are a few perceptions of key issues facing the nation, through the lenses of two notable politicians.

Political Leaders View the Future

Susan Page (1998) recently interviewed New Jersey Governor Christine Whitman, a two-term Republican, and Senator John Kerry of Massachusetts, a three-term Democrat to discuss their perception of key issues facing the nation as it nears the 21st Century. A summary of their responses presented at the annual meeting of the Association of National Advertisers in Naples, Florida include:

- Danger of retreat into isolationism.
- Global threats not just to the economy but in terms of ecology, terrorism and nationalism.
- Perception of foreign leaders that the U.S. is not a leader in a steadfast way. There is a need to educate the public to the U.S. role in the world—our responsibility. Senator Kerry noted that some 40 percent of the members of Congress do not have a passport, reflecting an outmoded parochialism. We need to get Americans to understand that foreign policy is not foreign anymore. "In my state, 30% of our economy is based on exports and that is true across our nation as we seek higher value-added jobs" said Senator Kerry.
- Governor Whitman sees the biggest challenge to our society as overcoming inherent fears of one another. She states that we have to learn to live with one another and celebrate our diversity.

- Kerry discussed race as a great divide in our nation. In the end he believes that problem will not be solved by affirmative action (although it can be helped by it) or by set-asides (though it can be helped by them). Kerry sees a need to be wary of how those programs are perceived in the broader cross-section of our country because we need a consensus to get important programs implemented.
- Whitman sees some danger to the Republic of powerful conservative groups including the Christian Coalition that require a litmus test on a social issue to be a member of a political party. She notes that there are wide diversities of opinions not only in the Christian community but in other religious and non-religious groups within our society.
- Both Whitman and Kerry have faith in technology gurus to solve the problems of loss of privacy and personal freedom in the computer information age.
- Whitman found that the two political parties have been the umbrellas, because each has a core set of beliefs in the middle and lots of interpretation around the edge.
- Kerry states that we are witnessing a generation tension in funding for education for the young versus social services for the aging.
- Both participants believed HMOs and managed care organizations would play a role in keeping health care costs down. Their original purpose was to cut the fat out of health care, making it more efficient, but reforms tend to move too far on one side and require a return to a more balanced approach (Page, 1998).
- Lee and Puente (1998) report that nationwide, eligible voter turnout was approximately 37 percent, the lowest since 1942. An increased population of women, Hispanics and other minorities will lead to major attention to their concerns, interests, and preferences by leaders of both political parties.
- Drinkard (1998) points out the biggest spenders reaped the rewards in elections. Drinkard notes that Larry Makinson, director of the nonpartisan Center for Responsive Politics, found that in 94 percent of the Senate races and 95 percent of the House races, the candidate who spent the most money won. Campaign financing may well be an issue in future elections.

A USA Today/CNN/Gallup poll conducted in the fall of 1998, found that of the population reporting to a telephone poll, the majority expected better race relations and availability of health care by 2025, while a majority expected worse moral values, increased crime and a deterioration in environmental quality. Other predictions were increased single-sex marriages, legalization of physician assisted suicide, most people doing their jobs and shopping from home, the Internet replacing stores (Page, 1998).

Newcomb (1998) discussed a recent Ford Foundation poll of registered voters that focused on opinions about multiculturalism on college campuses. She noted that recent decisions in California and Texas to reject race as a consideration in university admissions, as well as ongoing struggles at other schools make it a continuing issue for discussion and debate. The poll revealed that 66 percent of voters surveyed support college interventions to assure a diverse campus population. Over 88 percent of the respondents found a changing U.S. population requires diversity education that includes multicultural elements in the various disciplines. A majority of the respondents viewed higher education's purpose as teaching basic skills, career training, and preparation to work in a more diverse workplace. However, respondents were troubled with the possibility that emphasis on diversity might drive people apart and wondered whether there is a need for emphasis on common American values. Those who responded to the survey also wondered whether diversity education has a liberal political agenda and noted that while many schools have an emphasis on diversity, students tend to self-segregate (Newcomb).

Belsie (1998) revealed another future trend in the United States. The American economy created a stable working class, the mass middle class and now the world's first mass upper class has expanded. These are individuals who are not rich but earn at least $100,000 a year, spending it on waterfront vacations, sports-utility vehicles, and houses larger than their parents' homes were. David Frum, senior fellow at the Manhattan institute, a free market-oriented think tank in New York, identifies the growth of the economically comfortable population a new and emerging influence on the nation's economy. Belsie notes that this $100,000 plus club was 3.2 % of U.S. families in 1967 while it expanded to 11.8% of the population in 1997. The mass upper class population is usually made up of couples, two wage earners, well educated. Also with the growth in the mass upper class, billionaires have increased from 13 in 1982 to 179 in 1998. The Census Bureau,

Belsie states, reports that the share of people under the poverty line shrank a little between 1996 and 1997 but the poor are falling further and further behind today's mass upper class. This upper class can usually survive an economic downturn and provide a base for national economic stability.

Tomorrow's Child

Pat Wingert, Karen Springen, Elizabeth Angell and Michael Meyer (1998) teamed up to view the future. They reported on the following trends:

- Of the 3.9 million children born in America in the year 2000, 70,000 of them will still be alive in 2100.
- The millennium baby will be born into a nation of 275 million, third largest nation in the world with a projected population of 394 million by 2020. Three out of ten Americans will live in California, Texas, and Florida by 2025.
- The millennium baby will grow up in a country with a growing gap between the haves and have nots with growing disparities in wealth and income. Life expectancies will increase to 73 years for men and 80 years for women but minority men will average 64.6 years.
- Premature babies will be kept alive as early as 19-20 weeks after conception, some weighing eight ounces, with new techniques to allow them to breathe oxygen from a liquid solution until they can breathe on their own.
- Utero surgery will be viable in the next century with the help of tiny cameras mounted on needlelike probes.
- The child of the future will live in a time when the entire DNA of a normal person will be catalogued. Doctors will be able to diagnose

diseases in the utero and parents will decide whether to end the pregnancy.

- By the early years of the next century doctors will be able to cure disease by tinkering with patients' DNA. It may be possible, in combination with fetal surgery techniques to cure congential conditions even before birth through synthesizing normal copies of defective genes, altering genes that counteract it, and attach them to a vector such as a benign virus to carry them into a patients' cells.

- Kids in 2000 will have increased opportunities for universal pre-K education and the authors report that the new century will be a great time to be a child.

Turbak (1999) reported on baby's brain research that demonstrated humans who are simultaneously exposed to a pair of languages will separate the two and allow the child to speak each without a telltale accent. Further findings included the observation that children exposed to music at a young age often develop complex math, engineering and chess skills. Some child development experts believe future behavior characteristics for good or evil are laid down during this period. Childcare during the early years is vital for successful, satisfying, and full lives in adolescence and adulthood.

Evolving discoveries in health care, and gene manipulation will provide parents with potentially more healthy children. Problems in school safety, single parent families, latchkey kids, incivility, random violence, junk food eating, smoking, although being monitored more effectively will remain a challenge in the new century. Optional marriages will be on the horizon of the new millennium. The search for consensus, quality of life, and common community values will continue for the children of tomorrow.

Liberalism and Conservatism

The influences and forces that undermine essential unity within
diversity for a pluralistic democratic society are increasing. The far
right and far left function under an absolutistic belief system. Both
belief systems threaten the Aristotlean Golden Mean or balance on
which democratic systems must function. Current sexualMcCarthyism,
or the politics of scandal mongering, demonizing and criminalizing
political differences is an example of 17th Century Puritanism. Church
members watched and reported on other members' behavior in the 17th
century. Those guilty of perceived sins were hung or socially
ostracized. The Puritan *Commonwealth Act* of May 1650 focused on
the importance of suppressing the detestable sins of incest, adultery,
fornication through felonies, as well as the sentence of death. The act
elapsed in 1660 and was not renewed. As we approach the 21st century,
Puritanism is alive and well, as personal conduct and behavior is
subjected to public scrutiny and nationwide publicity. The terms
liberalism and conservatism are more difficult to define in our time as
there are degrees of both on a continuum. In the current political scene,
some see sexual McCarthyism as exposing politicians' infidelities
while others view it as a call for a higher standard of conduct. As
Puritans viewed their biblical state in terms of strict narrow
interpretation of the written works, so determined conservatives viewed
the Constitution in strict, narrow interpretation terms. Oliver Wendell
Holmes viewed the Constitution as something that should be broadly

interpreted to reflect the age in which events took place. Our social, political, and economic systems are different from that of the early Puritan Era. Paradigm shifts are often resisted as conservatives seek a return to the past which they believe represents an absolutistic ethical and moral system. While accusations about sex are part of American history, as witness Jefferson's and Cleveland's involvement with infidelity, today's exposure of sexual misconduct has become a means unto itself. Legislators from both parties are often engaged in political entertainment, posturing and theatre as witness the media circus in President William Jefferson Clinton's impeachment.

Feldman (1998) noted that while Richard Gephardt, Democratic minority leader called for an end to destroying imperfect people at the altar of an unattainable morality or fratricide, the rise of religious conservatism at the entrance of the 21st century has opened the door to demands for higher moral standards on all levels, public and private.

Calmes (1998) however, noted that the Clinton impeachment process, the first trial of a president since Andrew Johnson 131 years ago, along party lines reflects a struggle for power of the liberal and conservative political wings. The challenge for both political parties is the fringe element of both terms. These political fringe groups may exercise power out of all proportion to their numbers due to their powerful ideological and vocal support of a given side of an issue. Both parties have members that are increasingly familiar with how to use the media in the political process. Fringe groups have also mastered the art of lobbying Congress. Calmes viewed the issue of reflecting deeper changes in the nature of the political parties. Changes that emerge from regional party alignment, increasing precision in drawing congressional districts, declines in voter turnout that have magnified the influence of voters with strong ideological views. The chasm between the parties has been referred to as the most polarized at any time since the Reconstruction era in the late 1860s. Each Congressperson represents his voter base, regardless of national public opinion polls.

Calmes identified the power of this voter base by viewing the plight of Representative Mickey Edwards, an eight-term Republication from Oklahoma, who served in the G.O.P. leadership until ousted by a more conservative group. Edwards, an expert on the Constitution, now teaching at Harvard University, said he opposed impeachment because the charges against Clinton fall short of what's impeachable. Edwards admitted he might not be able to maintain that position in the House of

Representatives, in 1998, if he wanted to keep his Bible Belt seat and GOP leadership post. The same scenario could be made for the Democratic party with its base of labor union, minorities and blue collar workers who stress issues and lobby for programs beneficial to their political ends. Whatever the outcome, House of Representatives managers for the Senate impeachment trial were all male lawyers who used language overkill, ad hominem attack, hasty and overgeneralization, together with sophistry to sell their case to the 100 Senators. While corporations and universities have stressed the importance of implementing and encouraging diversity in the workplace to correspond to national demographics, Congress, with notable exceptions, remains in the reigns of males, predominately lawyers. Although there may be more evidence to come in the trial, at this writing the major thrust of the case involved sexual indiscretions with a White House intern and a history of such activity. It seemed at times during the impeachment process that conservative republicans were engaged in another form of a government shutdown equivalent to an earlier closing of government operations during another partisan crisis.

Polarization in Society

Several years ago David Mathews, currently President of the Kettering foundation, noted that Congress has difficulty finding areas of agreement in a fragmented society. He referred to Congressional gridlock. Tyson (1998) finds that Congressional appropriations have been completed on time only once in the past 15 years. One answer to the problem, is the inertia of Congress, a highly decentralized fragmented body with 435 Representatives and 100 Senators. A second cause for inertia is the tendency for Congressional members to attach items to appropriations based on the theory of bringing home the bacon to constituents. Third, appropriation bills are complex and huge. Few bills are read by Congresspersons, but summarized by unelected aides. Fourth, difficult decisions on areas to be funded are more difficult due to spending caps that were implemented in the mid 1990s. Congress tends to be oriented to investigations. Nixon's Watergate and Clinton's Monicagate illustrate the extent to which Congressional investigation has expanded with unelected lawyers and staff setting the tone for partisan bickering. So obsessed are Congresspersons with rules of procedure and legalese with a team of hired lawyers focusing on all sides of an issue, that major issues of concern to citizens are put on the back burner. Minority versus majority, seeking to win a point through one-up-man-ship to embarrass one another, engage in endless nitpicking and making mountains out of molehills. Grier (1998) reported the 105th Congress blocked or voted down campaign financing, antitobacco legislation, deregulation of the electric industry, banking deregulation, and health maintenance organization oversight. Reasons for the carnage include bad timing, personality and turf clashes, and political bumbling. The massive flow of paperwork makes it difficult if not impossible for members of Congress to keep up with legislative initiatives. Non-elected staff summarize the bills. At least 4,846 bills were introduced in the House while some 2,639 bills were introduced in the Senate during the 105th Congress.

Clymer, (1998) reported that there was little significant Congressional legislation in 1998 as the Republican Congress faced leadership weakness and instability as well as a preference for investigations of the president. Polarization between legislators and the White House reached a point where Senate majority leader Trent Lott criticized a joint chiefs of staff and U.S. intelligence recommended military operation in Iraq. Although Lott quickly reversed himself polarization between legislators and the President increased.

Serious issues are often too difficult and complex to address. For example, a key issue in 1998 is politicians of both parties who can't say no to rich people's soft money contributions. Marquez (1998) finds our democracy is threatened by loopholes in campaign finance laws which allow big money donors, such as corporations and labor unions, indirectly to finance election campaigns. Both major political parties pass that soft money to their candidates to get around individual-campaign legal limits. Marquez noted that the Senate voted down campaign-finance legislation in 1997 and 1998. He wonders if the American public lets fascination with thong bikinis, cigars and salacious up-against-the wall activities obfuscate the very real threat that unregulated soft money poses to our democracy. Senator Dale Bumpers (1998), retiring Arkansas Senator, noted that Congress has changed in the two plus decades that he has served in the Senate. The never-ending search for reelection campaign funds takes an increasing amount of time and energy. He decried the lack of civility in Congressional debates as well as polarization of the governing body. Bumper particularly stressed the threat to democracy of the exponential increase in funds necessary to run for election. In the 1998 elections more money than ever was raised by Congressional candidates while voter turnout of 36 percent was the lowest since 1942 (Wayne 1998). Wayne (1998) continued by noting that one theory to account for the trend was that while the amount spent on each vote was increasing, negative campaign advertising was turning off voters in ever increasing numbers.

Kissel (1998) reported on retiring Senator Dale Bumpers perceptions of government. Bumpers, 73 and a Democrat stepping down after 24 years in Washington, said he had grown increasingly frustrated with politics in recent years. He was particularly concerned about the amount of money it takes to run for reelection. Elections all depend on money and if the practice continues democracy will become unhinged and Bumpers said he has watched a terrible deterioration of the quality of the Senate during his tenure. Bumpers has seen six years of investigations into Arkansans since President Clinton's election in 1992 and many innocent people have been destroyed financially and mentally. He noted that you would have to go back to the Salem witchcraft trials to find anything comparable.

Ervin (1998) reported that sex lives of politicians are seen by the press as fair game. Rumors, inuendos, gossip, and accusations are part of the American political scene. Irvine found that Oklahoma reporters generally viewed sexual peccadillos as a personal matter and do not report them. Political opponents often use hate language in attacking one another. A case in point was Oklahoma State Senator George Miskovsky's accusation that David Boren was a homosexual. Miskovsky demanded that Boren state publicly whether he was a homosexual or bisexual. Boren, chief executive of Oklahoma, held a press conference and swore on a family Bible that he was neither a homosexual nor bisexual. Boren went on to win the governorship, to serve with distinction in the Senate and is currently President of the University of Oklahoma, Norman.

Harwood and Cummings (1998) reported that there has been a generation of scandal-driven American politics, in which partisan hatreds, an avid press corps and a hair-trigger independent counsel law have turned allegations of ethical misconduct into everyday weapons. Harwood and Cummings foresee a decline of polarized politics since the public seems to be turned off by constant political haranguing.

So polarized has Congress and Executive Branch become that the government was closed down in the past due to lack of appropriations approval. President Clinton's impeachment by Congress may be viewed as another form of a government shutdown as each of the political parties work to present their side of the issue to the public while ignoring the needs of citizens in areas of childcare, health care, and a multitude of other crucial issues. Although Congresspersons individually are tolerant and unbiased, collectively they often engage in exaggeration, half-truths, propagandizing the public through multimedia channels, and lying. Congressional zealots seem to take on the attributes of a lynching party with their investigative bent. Gridlock seems to be the result of the current fragmentation of our society.

Deutsch (1997) examines possible futures through his book *The Fabric of Reality*. He envisioned the future as being based on creating a continuous stream of new knowledge with a universe of a vast number of people interacting at many levels and in many different ways, but disagreeing. Perhaps like us in our time, future generations will not speak with one voice, will be mistaken in their assumptions and ends-in-view, and the culture will never be morally homogeneous. Deutsch continued by noting that people will be continually questioning assumptions that other people consider to be fundamental moral truths. He viewed the future world as comprised of a discordant yet progressive collection of overlapping communities. Perhaps the Congressional political turmoil with slash, burn and smear politics of the late 1990s will yet lead to a more compassionate, humane society in which people can resolve problems without a scorched earth policy of mutual distrust, antagonism, and continued one-up-man-ship.

Disenchanted Electorate

Gillman (1998) points out that voter apathy has been increasing. An estimated 4.6 million Americans failed to vote in the 1996 presidential election because they were too busy or couldn't take time off from work. That's a one in five potential voters surveyed and a three-fold increase over those who reported they didn't have the time to vote in 1980. Another 3.5 million registered voters didn't care about the political process or were frustrated with Washington politics, according to Lynne Casper, author of a report on the non-voters in America. Gillham reports that census records show a voter decline since 1964 when 69.3% of the population cast ballots compared to 54.2% in 1996. Women outvote men, and have done so since 1984. The greatest decline in voting was among the 18-24 year old population (Gillman). Costly attack ads in the media that stress negative real and imagined flaws of opponents, based on half-truths and fabrications, turn election campaigns into a circus-like atmosphere. Such a climate turns people off and increasing numbers of citizens are turned off and fail to vote.

Litigation

Millman (1998) noted that American workers must learn to play by new rules as recent rulings by the Supreme Court tighten regulations on individual behavior in the workplace. In August 1998 the high court found that if a person is fired, demoted or given an unpleasant reassignment as a result of spurning unwanted advances, the company is liable. This applies even if the harasser's conduct violated company rules or if senior management was unaware of the situation. It also applies even if no demotion or reassignment arose from the harassment. Thus not knowing is no longer a defense against harassment litigation. As Millman notes, employment lawyers and special interest groups are conducting training for sexual harassment prevention.

Stevenson (1999) noted that Texaco which settled a racial discrimination suit, due to tape recorded conversations of officials making disparaging remarks about blacks and discussing whether they should hide or destroy evidence, in late 1996 for $176 million, also settled a sexual bias suit in 1999 for $3.1 million The earlier settlement included the adoption of a program to promote equality, diversity and tolerance within the company while the later settlement covered 186 women employed between 1993 and 1996, in managerial and support jobs. These women were given $3.1 million in amounts of $1500 to $51,000 depending on length of employment and other factors. The $3.1 million settlement was the result of an audit by the Labor Department's Office of Federal Contract Compliance Programs in companies that do business with the Federal Government. Public Super Markets, one of the nation's largest food store chains, settled a discrimination lawsuit for $18.5 million in 1997. Unfortunately, some of these large settlements lead to employee morale problems, as employees who did not receive funds, and believe they are equally eligible, demonstrate their antagonism to those who received funds. Educational institutions at all levels, as well as the majority of corporations have sexual harassment policies in employment handbooks, ethics policies that employees must sign as well as Intranet and e-mail reminders. Due to ever-larger financial harassment settlements, caution must be used to prevent unverified and false claims of harassment.

Schmitt (1998) reported that in Esther Rodriquez vs. Mars Inc., maker of candy bars, Mrs. Rodriquez, a custodial worker at the Snickers plant in Chicago filed a federal sexual harassment lawsuit. Rodriguez, while under oath during the proceedings said she has spent time with her sick father, when in reality she was serving time in prison convicted of felony theft. Lying has become more common in both criminal and civil lawsuits in recent years.

Schmitt notes that in 1997 the National Law Journal, a newspaper for the legal profession found that hiding or destroying crucial court documents was one of the top new litigation trends.

In a government comprised of elected representatives most of whom are lawyers, it is easy to understand why partisanship, has in large part, led to a second term President being burdened with over $5 million in lawyer fees to defend himself against a variety of charges instigated by an independent counsel with unlimited funds, and unburdened by legalities that would restrict his prosecutorial zeal. In government as in the corporate sector, litigation has become a way of life. Cases of sexual misconduct are currently increasing at all levels of the judicial system and in all workplaces.

Taranto (1998) noted that the current sexual climate, in large part, was influenced by two Supreme Court Cases. *Meritor Savings Bank v. Vison (1986)* found sexual harassment was a form of discrimination actionable under Title VII of the Civil Rights Act of 1964, while *Miller v. California (1973)* defined the limits of obscenity law. Taranto noted that if Meritor and Miller unleashed ugly forces in American society, there are arguments that could be made in their favor. Taranto continued by finding that sex is a complicated, mysterious and deeply private matter, one that ought to be governed more by manners and morals rather than by laws. Harassment law is a poor substitute for decency, First Amendment absolutism a poor substitute for tolerance (Taranto, 1998). The search for civility and comity continues to be a challenge for the future.

Stepanek (1998) reported on the eagerness of lawyers to participate in the next litigation bonanza. She noted that legal seminars are already addressing the opportunities for the new millennium Y2K bug as we near the year 2000. So serious is the problem for companies that the Justice Department is offering immunity if companies collaborate on Y2K problems and President Clinton's crisis manager is trying to focus on fixing the problem to avoid liability problems. Stepanek reported that Congress is also considering national standards and special arbitration boards and a federal court to handle Y2K issues. Whenever, she continued, a date-dependent system is inaccurate because it hasn't been programmed to recognize dates after December 31, 1999, lawsuits are inevitable. Although the Social Security Administration's systems computers have been completely screened and adjusted for the Y2K problem because they started working on the problem in 1989, many other agencies and state systems have yet to be adjusted for the year 2000.

Burns (1998) expressed concern about vendor compliance, third party risk or supply-chain status since most major corporation and governmental agencies will be prepared for dealing with fixing computer systems to cope with the date change from 1999 to 2000. Large corporations are reprogramming or replacing millions of electronic brains to avoid mistaking the "00" for the last two digits of 2000 for the year 1900 while vendors, suppliers and smaller companies will be unprepared for the new century. Third party vendors' failure to deal with the Y2K issue could conceivably bring major corporate production to a halt. With efficiency management of just-in-time manufacturing, where supplies arrive at the moment they are needed, and no inventory on hand, even minor delivery interruption could idle a whole string of plants (Burns: 8 D).

Tannen (1998) wrote about litigation as war—a war of winning at all costs. Tannen found that while we look to our courts to reveal truth, the American legal system isn't designed to uncover truth. The legal system is about winning, even if it means coloring, distorting, or hiding facts to win. Tannen wrote that while lawyers have made major contributions in a number of areas such as civil rights, they have also sought to solve problems within a legal system that pits two sides against each other, letting them fight it out in public. Tannen concluded by noting that the American legal system assumes that truth emerges from polarized, warring extremes between lawyers. This adversarial system has led to a litigious society in which lawyers follow ambulances, recruit auto accident victims for lawsuits and seek out as many cases as possible. It is common to settle a winnable case out of court, rather than fight a prolonged costly legal battle to prove innocence. Some individuals make a lifelong occupation of filing lawsuits knowing individuals and corporations would rather negotiate a payment rather than get entangled in legal battles. Litigation is so pervasive in American society, that it places a heavy financial burden on individuals and corporations. The costly tobacco suit in the states and the federal government will be paid for by consumers for years to come. Lawyers are fighting over their share of the massive tobacco settlement.

Gullo (1999) reported that the federal government from 1990 through 1997 spent $378 million on counselors, judges and investigators who handle employee complaints. During the period another $488 million went to employees who won compensation awards ranging from a few thousand dollars to millions for class-action lawsuits. Civil rights complaints rose 70 percent from 17,000 cases in 1990 to nearly 29,000 cases in 1997, according to preliminary Equal Employment Opportunity Commission reports. Gullo continued by noting that although private firms have increased worker complaints, federal government employees use the grievance systems far more. Gullo found some of the rise in employee complaints is due to a 1991 law enabling federal employees to seek compensatory damages of up to $300,000 for discrimination. He also found some complaints are fraudulent. A postal worker complained she had a back injury that prevented her from working full hours. Postal investigators videotaped her running and bending at several dog shows while on paid leave. I am familiar with a case of a patient of a prominent neurosurgeon in South Florida who was sued for over $2 million for an ineffective operation. Private investigators found the patient jumping into the ocean from an expensive yacht. Litigation has permeated the American society and will continue in the future.

Affirmative action programs, often originated during court-ordered busing in the 1970s. These programs set aside a certain percentage of admissions for black and Hispanic students regardless of test scores. The programs were designed to provide equity in access to education and employment, but have recently come under legal challenges from students who were denied admission although they had high test scores and academic records. Affirmative action has been attacked at all levels of the educational spectrum in recent years. Bayles (1999) reported that one of the nation's oldest high schools, Boston Latin High School's, affirmative action program to encourage minority enrollment was found unconstitutional by a Federal appeals court. As in other cases Civil Rights groups encouraged Boston Latin High School administrators not to appeal the decision to the Supreme Court. They were fearful of more decisions more damaging to affirmative action programs nationwide. Affirmative action proponents believe future Supreme Court appointees may be more favorably disposed to such programs which encourage diversity and assist minorities gain access to education and employment opportunities.

Privacy in an Information Age

Rule (1998) pinpoints dangers to privacy by easy access to the World Wide Web. Personal data is sold by companies maintaining web sites. American Express is developing a venture with Knowledge Base to keep tabs on some 175 million Americans with the aim of selling reports on cardholders buying habits to merchants. Rule suggests more control over personal private information and ownership of one's own data. Access to e-mail, phone messages, and other communication networks illustrate the timeliness of "1984's" big brother concept.

Solomon (1998) tends to support a situational view of lying. He writes that all of those inappropriate questions from distinguished journalists, special persecutors, and the curious public deserve no answers, or an evasion or even a lie for an answer. Clinton's sex life and what he says about it do not have anything to do with Clinton's credibility or ability to govern (which are other questions altogether). A lie or an invitation to lie that is provoked by a breach of sacred personal boundaries is in moral limbo and no violation of public trust. As a philosophy Solomon (1998) finds that it is essential to distinguish between private and public life. Sex, with exceptions, is part of our private life. Lying about sex, while it may have significance for intimate relationships, has nothing to do with one's public credibility. In fact when publicly asked a rudely inappropriate question about one's private (adult, consensual) sex life, Solomon feels it is not only natural but even obligatory to lie, finesse, or refuse to answer. Future presidents will face continual invasions of privacy to the detriment of leadership effectiveness, if Congress and the media insist on detailing consensual sexual behavior through multimedia news channels.

Sexual Harassment

Novak (1998) reports that the Equal Employment Opportunity Commission was set up to protect employees who believe they are victims of certain kinds of discrimination based on sex, race, age, disability and is not a general mediation service. Individuals need to hire an attorney to gather facts and present the case for adjudication. Class action lawsuits are often easier to develop and settle than individual appeals. Belsie (1998) finds that if President Clinton were chief executive of a business, under increased surveillance by corporations, he would be fired. Corporate America is increasingly strict about sex in the workplace. What was acceptable in the 1980s is off bounds today. Belsie writes that many companies have been hit with a barrage of expensive judgments. In 1994 secretary Rena Weeks won a $3.5 million judgment against Baker & McKenzie law firm because one of its partners harassed her. Astra USA, a drug company, agreed to pay out nearly $10 million to women who had been harassed by senior executives. The Supreme Court has taken on three harassment cases in 1997 and two additional cases in 1998. One case deals with "quid pro quo" harassment where a supervisor asked for sexual relationships for increased salary and promotion. The other current case deals with a hostile working environment in which a woman is subjected to dirty jokes and salacious comments on her figure (Kilpatrick 1998). Federal courts have ruled women can sue employers if they feel they are and have been put in a hostile work environment.

Lardner (1998) reported that twenty years ago, sexual harassment was an undeveloped concept while at the portal of the 21st century it is the topic of over 15,000 complaints filed annually with the federal Equal Employment Opportunity Commission with an ever-expanding body of law. Mitsubishi Motor Company paid over $34 million to settle a harassment suit while Miller Brewing Co. fired an employee for telling his secretary about a suggestive episode of *Seinfeld*, a TV comedy show. A jury ordered Miller to hire the employee back and give him $26.6 million dollars. Lardner continued by noting that while half of all office romances end in lasting relationships or marriages such as Bill Gates and Melinda French, corporations, educational institutions, and governmental agencies, in fact all workplace managers, will have to be increasingly sensitive to possible lawsuits for harassment. Meanwhile sexual relationships will continue wherever men and women work in close contact for long periods of time. Enlightened corporate managers such as IBM will allow romantic relationships with a subordinate as long as one or the other moves to a different department. Lardner found that an increasingly common practice in anti-harassment policy is sensitivity training. This consists generally in a one or two hour case study approach with role-playing. Outside contractors, human resource staff, in-house attorneys are often used to teach managers and workers about the latest court decisions, the behaviors and words that might be offensive. Other techniques to deal with harassment issues include a 'love contract' stipulating that in spite of all risks, the individuals independently and collectively desire to undertake and pursue a mutually consensual social and amorous relationship (Lardner: 46). Senior citizens might view such a procedure as a turn-off to natural human sexual and companionship relations. Meanwhile between 6 and 8 million Americans enter into a romance with a fellow employee each year.

Landay (1997) discussed the Army leadership's attempt to deal with widespread sexual misconduct in the Army. Since many incidents of harassment occur in basic training, the army command is closely screening drill sergeant candidates, and overseeing the training atmosphere in the crucial three-week training program. Congresspersons have been seeking more values and sensitivity training in the Armed Services. Landay reported that Elaine Donnelly of the Center for Military Preparedness called for addressing the fraternization between senior and subordinate officers and at hearings to deal with the issue of harassment in the military, Donnelly reported a lot of testimony about female soldiers seeking special favors by giving sexual favors.

Kilpatrick also addresses the high employer costs of liability for harassment control, regulation, and sensitivity training sessions all of which increased costs for the consumers, shareholders, and workers. The Supreme Court also addresses the issue of whether school officials may be held liable for their failure to stop the sexual harassment of one student by another, an important issue for public school administrators. In the student-on-student harassment case, a fifth-grade girl in Macon, Georgia had endured groping and lewd remarks from a boy assigned to sit next to her in class. Parental complaints were ignored, the child's grades dropped and she thought about suicide. Her mother sued the school district, claiming that a 1972 federal education law protects students from sexual harassment by fellow students. A district court agreed but the decision was later reversed. If the Supreme Court holds that the education statute outlaws sexual harassment by fellow students, it may result in school districts nationwide being held liable if officials fail to act once a complaint is made. In addition it would broaden sexual harassment laws to cover a wider population of girls and young women (Richey 1998). Broadening laws in reference to sexual harassment may contribute to respect and civility for others and improve the quality of worklife in the future.

Kronholz (1998) relates the story of elementary teachers who offered love and consolation to any child who needed it. Even if students were dirty, I would hug them, one teacher related. Then, as is happening more frequently throughout the nation, two parents lodged abuse complaints against two teachers at her elementary school in New Jersey. One teacher had merely given a student a hurry-up pat on the back. Although both teachers were cleared, there were many conferences, investigations, and continual trouble. Now, the teachers will only give a half-arm hug, with two standing side-by-side and a teacher's aide in the same room. Affection will be shown by giving a child a pencil or a sticker. Kornholz continues by noting that in an era of heightened awareness of sexual abuse and escalating litigation, teachers' unions and some school districts are telling teachers, "don't touch", "don't pat", "don't tap" and definitely "don't hug". Pennsylvania's National Education Association Chapter publishes guidelines that urge teachers to do no more than "briefly touch" a child's arm or shoulder. New Jersey's chapter of NEA gives training seminars on what is and what isn't child abuse. Ohio's NEA chapter instructs teachers on how to give a non-hug, while Tennessee teachers union counsels students to disengage if a child initiates a hug.

A Missouri language arts teacher who admitted he consoled a "teary-eyed" eighth-grader with a hug, lost his job and was convicted of sexual harassment. The conviction was later overturned by a state of appeals court, but the personal fear, anguish, turmoil surely took a toll on the teacher. A spurious charge can end a teacher's life as he or she knew it. The New Jersey NEA affiliate says it defended a male music teacher in an investigation brought when an elementary school girl claimed sexual assault after the teacher helped her position her fingers on a musical instrument. Although the teacher was cleared, the investigation and the public embarrassment changed his life forever. He quit teaching (Kronholz, 1998). Although there are attempts to define and delineate legitimate and permissible nonsexual touching such as a coach hugging a student who made a goal or a kindergarten teacher's consoling hug for a child with a skinned knee, the threat to teachers, staff, coaches and administrators remain.

Meanwhile, *Education Week* (Hendrie 1998) reporters conducted a nationwide search through newspapers and computer data bases of active sexual cases involving teachers, coaches, and staff with students. Although there were many cases not reported by parents or students, the search turned up 244 cases, involving everything from unwanted touching to years-long sexual relationships and serial rape. Abuse was found in all educational settings—public and private, religious and secular, rural and urban, rich and poor. The setting was in the school building itself—everywhere from closets and classrooms to showers and stairwells—or off campus in cars, motel rooms, school buses, or at the student's or employee's home. Students targeted for abuse are often least inclined to report the offense and the least likely to be believed if they do. Often abused students have difficulty at home, may come from single parent families and are attracted by an authority figure telling them they are needed and appreciated. Often when abused students reported their sexual activities with a popular teacher, friends turned against them becoming outcasts in their schools and communities. Hendrie reported that suspects ranged from 21 to 75 years old with an average age of 28. More than seven out of 10 were teachers, but principals, janitors, bus drivers and librarians were among the accused. Although most sexual offenders were men, over 20 percent were women. Students ranged from kindergartners to high school seniors, with two-thirds of the cases involving female students and about one-third involving boys. Often, Hendrie continued, by reporting that in over two-thirds of the cases, students were of high school age—14 years or older. Coaches, drama or music teachers represented at least one-third of those involved in student sex abuse, suggesting additional opportunities for closer relationships in settings such as locker rooms, activity offices, rehearsal rooms and road trips (Hendrie, 1998). Zero tolerance for sexual relations between school teachers, administrators and staff has been implemented in many school districts.

Davis v. Monroe County Board of Education (1994) is an interesting case currently before the Supreme Court which may rule on it by the summer of 1999. Briefly, the U.S. District Court found that sexually harassing behavior of a fellow student was not covered by Title IX. La Shonda, a fifth grade student, was subjected to repeated harassment by a boy, G.F., who was seated next to her. La Shonda notified her classroom teacher who assured her the principal had been notified. After continued harassment Ms. Davis the girls mother notified a board superintendent of the problem. Meanwhile La Shonda's grades fell and she was subjected to emotional and mental stress. The boy reported repeatedly fondled La Shonda's breast, grabbed her crotch and exposed her to verbal sexual abuse. Ms. Davis charged the school with discrimination when it disciplined G.F. for striking a white female student and not for harassing La Shonda, a black female. The mothers complaint dealt with the due process clause of the 14th Amendment alleging that La Shonda was deprived of her liberty interest in being free from sexual harassment on intrusions on her personal security. The District Court for the Middle District of Georgia found that state had no constitutional duty to protect its citizens from private persons. The District Court held that section 1983 liability attaches only when the state breaches an affirmative duty which it owes to its citizens. Ms. Davis also stated that the classmate's advances violated Title IX, but the court held that Title IX was not a basis for a cause of action in this case.

On appeal to the 11th Circuit Court of Appeals (1996), by a 2-1 decision, the *Davis v. Monroe* lawsuit against the district was reinstated. The Appeals Court found that under Title IX of the Education Amendments of 1972 (Title IX prohibits discrimination in those institutions which receive federal assistance), a school district can be sued for money damages if school authorities knew about but failed to act on a "sexually hostile education environment" created by student-to-student sexual harassment. The appeals court found that although sexual harassment doctrine has generally developed under Title VII (Civil Rights Act of 1964 which forbids discrimination in public and private employment on the basis of race, color, national origin, religion and sex), the guidelines seem equally applicable to Title IX. Ms. Davis is seeking $1 million in damages against the 3,500 school districts in Forsyth, near Macon, Georgia. The full U.S. Court of Appeals for the 11th Circuit in a 1997, 7-4 decision, upheld the original District Court's dismissal of the Davis family's lawsuit, finding that school districts are not able to control the behavior of students as they are employees. Other appeals courts have ruled districts can be sued under Title IX. The sexual harassment law is still emerging and federal courts have diverse rulings on the issue of student-to-student harassment. The Clinton administration supported a review of the issue by the Supreme Court and has published a booklet, *Protecting Students from Harassment and Hate Crimes, A Guide for Schools.* Henry (1999) reported that FBI crime statistics show that over 8,000 bias motivated crimes occurred in 1997 with 848 of those in public schools roughly half in K-12 and half in college.

The Supreme Court, on appeal, took the case. A decision is expected by July of 1999. Early reports suggest members of the high court are questioning plaintiff's lawyers about the national propensity or tendency of boys and girls to tease one another and are indicating some problems ought to be dealt with at the local school level. Although the Supreme Court members have not yet ruled on the case, early indications are that they are concerned about opening up a kettle of worms. If students and their parents are able to receive tort damages for harassment from school districts, it would put a heavy burden on school finances already restricted. School officials throughout the country have written policies about appropriate student behavior distributed to all employees, parents and students. These policies identify what sexual harassment is, steps that can be taken to prevent it and channels for reporting such incidents while maintaining confidentiality. Recent Supreme Court cases suggest strong support for the historical concept of *loco parentis* wherein school authorities stand in relationship to pupils as does a parent or guardian. School authorities are given power and authority to maintain safe schools and to take such steps as deemed necessary to provide an environment conducive to learning. There are no easy answers to student-to-student harassment but seeking ways to encourage, or instill student respect for one another, and requiring codes of conduct in both theory and practice are initial steps to addressing the issue. Parental involvement when possible, community initiatives when parental involvement is not possible are essential steps to addressing these student challenges.

While educational reformers and their reports stress accountability, efficiency, achievement goals for standardized tests, longer school days, longer school years, increased stress on academic achievement in college preparation courses in math, language arts, reading, the sciences, and the liberalizing liberal arts, and computer skills, there is little written about the challenge of litigation excesses to academic freedom as well as to the organizational climate necessary for learning and teaching to take place.

To point out the dangers of excesses in litigation facing educators in our time does not diminish the need to be alert to child abuse. Holmstrom (1998) noted that the National Committee to Prevent Child Abuse reported that 14 out of every 1,000 children in the US were substantiated as victims of maltreatment in 1996. Six out of every 1,000 children under 18 in the US. are now in foster care. But, as Holmstrom points out, the complexity of some cases is illustrated by the plight of one mother on cocaine. She had had her first child at 14, then three more while living with a violent boyfriend. Her neglected children were taken from her and placed in a foster home. With a different man, an alcoholic, she had a fifth child, born prematurely and placed in foster care. Often such children who live in dysfunctional families seek love and affection from their teachers, coaches and staff. Their parents may then engage in litigation due to anger at their situation in marriage, the job market, drug abuse, and social alienation.

Although federal court decisions vary depending on the make-up of the court, facts in the case, and the Zeitgeist or spirit of the times, a recent Wisconsin case (Nabozny v. Podlesny, 1996) of anti-gay harassment led to absolving the school district but holding school administrators responsible for failing to protect a student from abuse by his peers. Three Ashland Public School District's administrators were held liable by the court for not creating a safe environment for homosexual students and the school district agreed to pay a $ 1 million out-of-court settlement to a student who allegedly suffered years of anti-gay harassment. The Ashland, Wisconsin School District's insurance company will pay most of the settlement. The Nabozny v. Podlesny case suggests that school administrators need to be kept informed of student complaints about harassment and should have known about such activity. Eugene Volokh, a Constitutional law professor at the University of California, Los Angeles, believes administrators need to take a more aggressive stance toward student-to-student harassment. School administrators should try to stop student-on-student harassment through reprimand, involving parents, or expelling or transferring the harasser. Initiatives for corrective action need to be implemented. Faculty and staff need to be informed of the schools harassment initiatives and policy since there may be a tendency among counselors and faculty to cite confidentiality as a reason for failing to notify administrators of harassment cases and incidents. School districts need to add sexual orientation to their school policy publications, create a safe environment for pupils, support student efforts for peer support and provide training for faculty and staff to serve the needs of all students including gay and lesbian ones (*Your School and the Law*, 1997).

Excesses in litigation settlements reflect the materialistic aspects of society. Individuals seek ever larger settlements encouraged by lawyers eager for fees.

Growing anger is reflected in more severe violence in schools and society. It is seen in driving patterns, parental distrust of teachers, administrators and staff, hate crimes, and in media obsession with any story that can sell. Media elites are not averse to spinning or enlarging a story. Some reporters have even been dismissed due to falsifying news for a great story that sells.

Economic Power Elites

Our democracy operates through Congressional lobbying. Power elites create a bond, perhaps essential, between government and business/industry. However, excessive risk-taking may result in unforeseen multiplier effects. While millions of investors can be enriched or impoverished by fluctuations in stock markets, the wealthy are often provided bailout protections. An example is the bailout of the Long-Term Capital Management, a large hedge fund. Bailouts total over $3.165 billion. Fraser (1998) wonders whether financial executives with their own money invested in the hedge fund were really saving the global economy or their own interests. The unprecedented rescue September 23, 1998 of the Long-Term Capital Hedge fund was orchestrated by the Federal Reserve Bank of New York. Regulators were worried that the hedge fund would be forced to dump its massive portfolio of bonds on the market, causing prices to fall, interest rates to rise and rattling investor confidence around the world (p. B 9). Brandon (1998) suggests the Long Term Capital Management bailout raises some serious policy questions that may have significant foreign policy implications. The main question might be: How can the United States officials speak with a straight face to Asians about "moral hazard" when US authorities do the exact opposite of what they preach. Brandon defines "moral hazard" as the temptation by financial institutions and banks to make risky loans and investments on the assumption they will be bailed out if they fail. While the bailout was based on fear that the hedge fund would unsettle world financial markets, Asians view the bailout as proof of U.S. self-interest in protecting its own system.

Brandon notes that when the financial crisis in Asia was spreading, the U.S. and the International Monetary Fund extolled the virtues of non-intervention in the economy to let market forces decide, while some Asian leaders blamed hedge funds for their economic meltdown. Brandon continues his analysis of financial markets by noting the people who ran Long Term Capital Management kept their jobs and received a fee on their rescue fund while 2,000 people in Thailand were losing their jobs each day. The situation was the same in Indonesia and other Asian countries. Sirico (1998) however, finds the hedge fund meltdown to be a human, not an institutional failure. Sirico finds that whenever there are high-profile hedge fund failures, the old charge of capitalist greed arises. He continues by noting that financial problems arise when arrogance tempts us to believe in our own infallibility and it is this hubris that leads some intellectuals to embrace the folly of central planning. Sirico finds that no economic system can rid the world of human infallibility and none should try.

Barlett and Steele (1998) reported on Corporate Welfare, which is defined as any action by local, state or federal government that gives corporations or an entire industry, a benefit not offered to others. Barlett and Steele noted that the Federal Government spends $125 billion a year in corporate welfare. They found that two years after Congress reduced welfare for individuals and families, corporate welfare continues to expand, infiltrating every part of the American economy. While some companies fend for themselves, large corporations with political influence receive freebies through what are often called "economic incentives", "empowerment zones, or "enterprise zones" and according to Barlett and Steele, this creates an unfair playing field for those left out of government largess. Karmatz and Labi (1998) found that clever companies are increasingly pitting politicians against one another in the cause of better and bigger tax breaks. In the end, Karmatz and Labi found that rarely does corporate welfare create jobs and the incentives often rob government coffers of funds that could be used for the public good. Those of us who have worked with the Agency for International Development programs are familiar with efforts by various third world agencies and governments to stimulate competition for more resources between and among United

States overseas worker teams. Each team tries hard to live up to the expectations of third world power elites for more resources. The same process is in effect when American city, state, regional and national corporations threaten to go elsewhere with new plants and jobs if they don't receive enough corporate welfare.

Meanwhile, the United States for the first time in its history is a debtor nation with an implication for the future of the nation's economic health. Growing trade imbalances with other nations may be detrimental to future financial stability, but on the other hand, these imbalances may be important contributors to bailing out nations in financial distress. The United States, an overproducing nation, has to maintain its foreign markets even if it means maintaining a negative foreign trade balance.

Quintanilla (1998) points out, after months of low unemployment and intense competition for workers, U.S. companies are preparing for a widespread round of year-end job cuts. Although evidence of an emerging recession is missing, people laid off from their jobs may find it difficult to find a job as good as their former one. Much of the job growth in the U.S. has been mainly in low-wage occupations such as retailing, temporary labor and food service. Diane Swonk, deputy chief economist at BankOne noted that when there are tight labor markets in the U.S., and no ability to raises prices easily, the solution is to fire 1,000 or more people as was done by many U.S. companies in the fall and winter of 1998.

Garten (1998), Dean of the Yale School of Management notes that companies implementing cost-saving layoffs may please Wall Street, but at the same time can destroy morale and productivity. Companies, he continues, that survive in a highly competitive and changing global marketplace, must place a premium on extreme flexibility, built-in contingency planning, and intensive focus on developing new skills for management and the workforce.

System breaks or unexpected events such as the financial market melt downs in Russia, Brazil or Asia can lead to market turmoil. Export and import trade imbalances are essential as corporations try to seek, maintain and expand new markets for their goods. As Garten reported, companies need to be able to shift product sales to growth areas rapidly. He used Toyota as an example of a rapid response auto-maker that standardized models for efficient production as well as retooled factories so that they can serve local markets as well as exporting to growth markets.

The boom and bust economic cycles are a continuing challenge to economic and social stability. These cycles continually challenge governmental officials and agencies to find ways to provide a social protective network for the underemployed, unemployed, and at-risk populations.

Have and Have Not Populations

Holt (1998) discusses the result of the worldwide population explosion. From 1950-1995 the world population doubled from 2.5 billion to 5.7 billion. United Nations researchers find that if the fertility rates remain the same there will be over 57.2 billion people in 2100 and some 296.3 billion in 2150. A real challenge is the distribution of the population with industrialized nations having the same 1.1 billion population in 2050 as in 1995, while the rest of the world will have a population explosion from 4.6 billion to 13.9 billion. The industrialized world has too few young people while the third world has too many. In the United States, Japan and Europe these population imbalances threaten health care systems. Holt notes that Italy has more people over the age of 60 than under the age of 20. These population figures lead to intense pressure to emigrate from third world countries to industrialized nations in pursuit of a better life. Massive population shifts will lead to changing ethnicity. Entering into a new millennium in Western Europe and the United States, industrialized nations will face a change in demographics as minorities come closer to being majorities or significantly greater percentages of the population (Holt, 1998). Higher standards of living, better social services networks, and higher paying jobs lead to increased flows of third world illegal immigrants being smuggled into Western Europe and the United States. In addition, American embassies throughout the world are inundated with citizens seeking to study, or emigrate to the United States for a better life.

Sklar (1998) reported on a 1997 survey of hunger and homelessness in 29 cities. Results of the survey found that nine out of ten cities regularly deny homeless families shelter due to inadequate resources. There are long waiting lists for affordable childcare; and with time limits for moving from welfare to work, states are moving welfare recipients off welfare even if they can't find work or childcare. Single mothers with limited job skills often earn too little to have health insurance. Although there are government initiatives to deal with the problem, the need for health insurance is for lower wage earners or self-employed unskilled workers remains to be met. Sklar pointed out that former welfare recipients typically earn less that $10,000 a year, not enough to support a family, and adding to the ranks of workers not earning a living wage. Meanwhile, as Sklar reported, the federal government spends some $125 billion a year of tax dollars on corporate welfare. That amount is more than the federal government spent in 1994 on Aid to Families with Dependent Children, Supplemental Security Income, food programs, housing benefits, education aid, childcare, job training, the Earned Income Tax Credit and other programs serving low-income people.

Marian Wright Edelman (1998) a lifelong advocate for children at risk and in need, reported that every 10 seconds in America, a child is reported abused or neglected. The National Coalition for the Homeless reports that at any given time 1.1 million children are living in emergency shelters. About 5 million older children are alone after school. They lack supervision and support for their school-work. Latch-key children are a special challenge for our communities and educators. The Children's Defense Fund works to improve children's lives and is an advocate for improving opportunities and health care for those in need. Their basic philosophy includes the goal of having every child receive a health start, a head start, a fair start, a safe start and a moral start in life (CDF, 1998). The Children's Defense Fund put the challenges for American children in perspective in *The State of America's Children Yearbook 1998.*

The State of America's Children Yearbook 1998.
1 in 2 preschoolers has a mother in the labor force
1 in 2 will live in a single-parent family at some point in childhood
1 in 2 never completes a single year of college
1 in 3 is born to unmarried parents
1 in 3 will be poor at some point in childhood
1 in 3 is a year or more behind in school
1 in 4 is born poor
1 in 4 is born to a mother who did not graduate from high school
1 in 4 lives with only one parent
1 in 5 lives in a family receiving food stamps
1 in 6 has a foreign-born mother
1 in 7 has no health insurance
1 in 8 is born to a teen-age mother
1 in 8 never graduates from high school
1 in 11 lives at less than half the poverty level
1 in 12 has a disability
1 in 13 is born at low birth weight
1 in 25 lives with neither parent
1 in 132 dies before age 1.
1 in 680 is killed by gunfire before age 20 (*The State of America's Children Yearbook,* 1998)

Many American schools have childcare provisions for unwed teen-age mothers and fathers. The babies ride on the school buses with their teen parents. The teen parents attend classes for high school GED or a high school diploma. They take breaks from classes to learn how to be a parent in the childcare centers located on the school grounds. Frequently the childcare centers receive extra support from civic organizations such as Kiwanis and other community outreach groups. There have been more teen-age fathers attending parenting classes in recent years. Another nationwide trend is single fathers raising families and increasingly grandparents are raising their children's children.

Jackson (1999) found that even in the midst of a strong economy, four out of ten welfare recipients or 38 percent of the group are unemployed. Although, as Jackson pointed out, progress has been made in finding jobs for welfare recipients, the *Children's Defense Fund and the National Coalition for the Homeless* reported that only 28.8 percent had wages above the poverty level, while 51 percent had wages that did not even reach 75 percent of the poverty level. Jackson found that there is a continuing need to generate sustaining jobs particularly in urban poverty centers. The nation's poor will continue to need governmental safety net programs in the new century.

Future Workplaces

Challenger (1998) identifies snapshots of tomorrow's workplace. Motorola engineers will work closely with students to solve real engineering problems and attract more students to the field of engineering. Challenger finds a future economy with worker shortages created by consumer demand and an employment population too small to meet demands for workers. Workers may place ads "situation wanted" on the Internet and find employment. The U.S. Bureau of Labor Statistics projects 151 million jobs by 2006 with some 141 employed. To attract highly productive workers, creative enticements will be offered in the future including opportunities to work in home or other than traditional workplace environments. Exercise and stress reduction programs may be offered to retain and maintain the health of employees in the future. Employers will need to seek a balance between junior and senior workers with a generation X as well as baby boomers in between the two groups.

Challenger also finds employers will need to find ways to socialize workers who are isolated in their homes. Part-time, and temporary workers will be increasingly used in the future as corporations face demands to be flexible in order to eliminate or expand operations according to needs and changes in the marketplace. Romanos (1998) noted that employers need to consider alternative work forces a new genre of employee who isn't owned by the company. Different people may work at different times. Developing a bank of trained workers who are available for high-activity periods or off-hours, and who may be working at other companies, is an example of an alternative workforce. These workers may be recruited from asking existing workforce to seek help from friends, family, business associates or scouting local schools for assistance in finding workers to fill niche positions on an as-needed basis. Romanos continued by suggesting other sources of an alternative workforce may be found among retired people and women returning to the workforce. With Americans working harder than ever and trying to integrate their lifestyles with work, alternative workforce benefits both worker and employer.

Forman (1998) reported corporations including Xerox, Coors Brewing, Mobil Oil, American Express and Nations Bank, and over 350 other companies, in order to recruit and retain workers, are offering health insurance for same-sex domestic partners, opposite sex partners, tax dependents including parents, siblings, adult children, aunts and uncles. Forman found that as global competition increases and 2000 approaches, few corporations want to lose a potential superstar to a competitor's more accommodating benefit plan.

With a global marketplace in perpetual change, tension and adjustment, major corporations will have to be able to shed, transfer, re-train workers. Organizational paternalism and worker loyalty to their employers are becoming extinct or seriously eroded. Irwin (1998) noted that where monolithic giants once offered lifetime employment for loyal workers, downsizing has become an acceptable, often desirable, element of strategic planning. Job-hopping has emerged as a way for the American worker to respond to massive downsizing, reengineering, restructuring, and as a way to prosper and build an attractive resume. Armour (1998) pointed to another wave of the future in corporate America. Ford Motor as well as other companies are offering voluntary retirement severance plans to shed low performing employees. Many employees, not wanting to retire fear being laid off with no benefits if they do not accept buy-out. Employers avoid lawsuits by making workers sign agreements not to sue and agreeing that they accepted the buy-outs voluntarily. Such buy-outs of employees labeled as poor job performers can lead to morale problems. Workers often wonder what criteria and who within the organization gathers data that are used to eliminate co-workers. Armour noted that severance plans for those employees labeled as non-performing is often done quietly on an individual basis.

Coolidge (1998) discussed the role of annual performance reviews which is a powerful tool to influence employee performance but also one of the most scorned, reviled, disparaged tools in the management job. A 1997 survey of 1700 human resource specialists revealed that only 5 percent were satisfied with the review process which is often hampered by politics and is of little value to workers. With downsizing, a top ranked individual can be fired or laid off. Self-appraisal has been helpful in conjunction with supervisor ratings. Performance reviews utilized to assist an employee to improve performance, can be valuable tools. Higher education institutions formerly used performance reviews for instructional improvement. The current trend in higher education is to use these reviews to determine salary distribution and too often reviews are based on internal power politics.

Many individuals should not accept buy-outs but may be informed by management that if they don't take the severance package and sign a statement that they are taking it voluntarily and that they will not sue the company, no incentives will be offered in the future. This devious action may lead to distrust of management. The severance packages occur not only in corporations but in other institutions, including universities. The device is often used to get rid of higher paid employees who are replaced with entry level workers. Maharaj (1998) reported that even in a good economy, laying off workers has become as routine as dumping old computer hardware. By October 1998, in the first ten months of the year there were some 523,000 job cuts, mostly from the domestic workforce. Senior managers under pressure from Wall Street for quick, consistent profits, often take the easiest way out by reducing employment costs. Maharaj also referred to a just-in-time employment practice where temporary workers, and throw away executives meet company needs on a contingency basis. They are laid off when a job is completed.

Companies may hold inventories for a long time, but employees will not be retained for one minute more than they are needed. Maharaj noted that corporate executives indicate a need to have the flexibility to cut and rearrange their workforces to maintain competitiveness. Other workforce changes include throw away executives who are brought in to solve a problem on a temporary basis. Many management employees have been rehired after they were fired or laid off as consultants for specific assignments. In the era of downsizing, some corporations find they have fired or laid off too many middle management employees and seek to rehire them to fill a void in company operations. Such rehired employees tend to seek increased salaries and have a reduced sense of organizational loyalty. Research university managers tend to follow corporate models in reducing senior level faculty ranks and formulating new policies to allow for hiring individuals in areas with growth potential. Munk (1999) revealed a new trend in corporate America particularly in technology. She reported that it is hard to find a job in business at 55, but in rapidly changing technology fields, employees at 40 are starting to look and feel old in the job arena. A category for professional minorities include those aged 40 and over. Age groups can rise to the top but right behind them is another generation ready to take over. Munk reported that a young software engineer lost her job after 14 years. She sent out 300 resumes, got four phone interviews, one in-person interview and not a single job offer. At 44 the young engineer with a 1983 Masters Degree from the University of California at Irvine with 23 years of experience who had moved into management when forty-something managers are a dime a dozen, was jobless. She had to decide whether to go back to school or take a job with a lower salary. Meanwhile people half her age were better qualified in technical skills, better at learning new skills, younger more flexible and adaptable. The software engineer found herself at 44, out of work and useless. Typical of the feelings of forty year olds being replaced by twenty year olds was "after all I have done, and all I have worked, and have never taken a day off for sick leave in over twenty years, it doesn't mean a thing". Such responses reflect a broad spectrum of the nation's workforce at the door of a new century.Munk noted that from the manager's perspective, for half the salary ($40,000-$50,000) I can get a smart, raw kid who will work 7 days a week for me. I'll train him the way I want him, he will grow with me and I'll pay him long-term options so I own him. He will do exactly what I want and if he doesn't I will fire him. The manager continued by noting that the alternative is an improperly trained forty-year-old that I will pay twice as much for half the work. In addition, the forty-year-old will not listen to what I say. This type of mentality has permeated our managerial class from corporate, to university, to private sector leaders. Dallas (1999) found that some 60-75% of jobs of the future will require technology skills with 75% of the transactions between individuals and government becoming electronic. She concluded by noting that access equity will be the civil rights issue of the 21st century. Cyber-communities will need to have the intervention of government social network agencies to provide for those who have been disconnected from their jobs through age and need for knowledge updating.

Irwin cited Barbara Rudolph's Free Press book *Disconnected* to describe a changing labor force that finds restlessness and emotional detachment to be an asset. Some individuals who have been laid off due to downsizing are able to adjust, while others engage in self-destructive behavior and often are unable to remain in a stable marriage. The ruthless dismissal from a job is a deeply emotional experience for those who have invested a lifetime in a career. Sunbeam Corporation's chief executive was referred to as "Chainsaw Al" who used deep workforce reductions for bottom line results. Sunbeam's new chief executive is trying to save 4,000 jobs that would have been lost under "Chainsaw Al Dunlap's" restructuring and downsizing policy. Dunlap's strategy of firing workers, downsizing, and restructuring, successful in the past, failed with Sunbeam and he was fired for failing to increase profits.

A new young employee of Sunbeam's Neosho, Missouri plant reported that whole sections of the plant were empty, chairs and desks piled up. She found morale so poor that the few senior workers still left would find devious ways to reroute work from new hires to themselves in an effort to keep their jobs. Meanwhile new employees were placed in a difficult position, not having authority to challenge these devious acts, often left the organization after working but a short time. Numerous incidents occur of top-flight workers, in the nation's most prestigious corporations, having to face leadership changes which often lead to loss of self-esteem, individual dignity, morale and worth.

Chief executive officers often delegate power to individuals unable, or unwilling to properly supervise those plant managers under their areas of control. Management changes can lead to frustrated, unmotivated, alienated employees. When a sensitive, well-qualified, top-flight worker is faced with Machiavellian type manager after a considerable length of time working in a collegial, humane environment, severe health problems may result. Although most workers adjust to a hostile working environment, the author is familiar with cases in which the employee became so engrossed with the unfairness, unpredictability, irrationality, and deviousness of her supervisor, that the young woman, after sleepless nights attempted suicide.

Cases of devious management initiatives to get rid of tenured faculty in major universities are not uncommon. Giving little if any pay increase, assigning off campus classes often 400 round trip miles from the institution, moving faculty from their offices, assigning a work overload, using various forms of social ostracism, often are initiatives taken to get rid of tenured faculty members. Most faculty members leave without protest, a few sue, and some stay on until retirement. Part-time and adjunct faculty are subject to termination without notice regardless of their productivity, efficiency or contribution to the organization. Machiaevellian employee manipulation is not limited to faculty, it occurs at all levels of university administration as well through a process of musical chairs—moving people from one office to another with little, if any, notice, or what is more common, shifting administrators to faculty positions with their administrative salary intact. So prevalent is office politics in central university administration that new administrative hires from the chancellor on through middle management, seek and are granted a tenured position, often a full professorship, within a college. Universities as well as corporations and businesses, often have a negative work culture. When university chief executive officers are dismissed by boards of trustees, they are often given a distinguished tenured professorship in a college. These factors may not occur in unionized institutions, although problems exist in those institutions as well.

Subtle forms of age, race, gender, and ethnic discrimination are faced by millions of workers whose life-time investments in a job are trashed for the purpose of bringing in new blood, new ideas, cost-effective younger workers. Few laid off workers litigate due to age, sex, gender or racial discrimination. Many workers have too much pride and self-esteem, as well as fear of being known as a troublemaker in future job searches. Cunniff (1998) reported on a survey released by Kepner-Tregoe, a management consulting firm, that found worker dissatisfaction is widespread and growing. Increased worker turnover, loss of key personnel, poorer product quality and service, inadequate worker-management communication, not feeling valued, inadequate income, were a few findings of the survey. These findings come at a time when jobs are plentiful and incomes are rising faster than inflation. Kepner-Tregoe concluded their research by questioning whether management is contributing to a solution or is part of the problem.

Shellenbarger (1999) pointed to corporate inability to deal with employee grieving problems associated with the death of a loved one. A top flight woman employee whose brother died in her arms, asked her boss for a two hour lunch break once a week to attend a support group for grieving siblings. Although she worked 50-hour weeks and had been promoted three times in as many years, her boss insisted she take vacation time and four months later fired her. Some corporations have developed policies to support employees in crisis. Shellenbarger found that managers need training in responding to grievance issues and co-workers should react openly and compassionately. In hectic work environments, when an employee cannot carry his or her workload, it places a challenge on managers and co-workers to handle the issue. Division and department managers' humaneness and sensitivity to challenges facing workers is an important ingredient in healing processes. Other areas of challenge are alcoholism, sexual relations between supervisors and employees, chronic complaining, and lack of knowledge and ability to carry out job assignments. When an employee fails to carry a workload, others have to pick it up. Dismissing an employee or giving negative recommendations, in a litigious society has to be handled with caution, sensitivity, and if possible with some guidance and counseling. In many instances, officials pass the buck to subordinates, so they will not have to handle employee firing. Inadequate or poor employee performance, alcoholism, drug use, attitude problems, or absenteeism, is often not reported on recommendation forms due to possible litigation. Often accurate, truthful employee appraisals are given over the phone but with a trend to tape record conversations, the avenue may be limited.

McLaughlin (1998) finds Americans are working harder, and more hours without taking a break. More workers are balking at forced overtime through more strikes and other forms of protest. Corporation executives who have reduced their workforce, are operating with fewer employees who are required to do the same or more work than when the corporations were fully staffed. Workers average enough extra hours to equal about three more weeks of work per year than they did just 10 years ago. McLaughlin finds some economists are predicting a period of adjustment over the issue of overtime. Eventually that adjustment could mean additional salary, or less time at work. Workers face a feast and famine phenomenon in the workplace, complaining about overtime but with falling wages and job insecurity, they often do it. Dale Brickner, an emeritus labor professor at Michigan state University sees increased labor strife resulting from being pushed too far. Corporate America finds overtime cheaper than hiring and training new workers (McLaughlin, 1998: 1,11). Rutledge (1998) noted that we have trained an entire generation of managers to make money by firing people and restructuring balance sheets. Rutledge further found that there is a shortage of broadly trained operating managers good at product development and marketing rather than cost cutting. In a tight labor market in the United States, unless there is a significant downturn in the economy, employers will no longer be able to increase earnings by firing people. Operating managers may be increasingly valuable.

Armour (1998) notes that employers are losing millions of dollars as unscheduled absences reach their highest levels in seven years. Some $4 million a year is being lost due to absenteeism in large corporations, a 32% jump since 1997. Armour finds part of the reasons for growing absenteeism include increased work demands, low unemployment which may be a temporary state of affairs, work induced stress, and employers asking workers to give 110 percent since reduction in force have cut available employees. Some corporations, to meet workers needs and cut down on absenteeism, are providing childcare centers with nurses for youngsters with health needs, as well as alternative flexible work assignments. A growing number of corporations are providing and/or supporting commuter schools for working parents. Business and corporations provide some funding, supplies and support services for commuter schools and in return have less employee absenteeism, tardiness and more dedicated employees. These schools on or near workplaces, provide opportunities for parents to check on their children during their workdays. Critics of such commuter schools reported that they provide an unfair advantage to some kids but not others whose parents do not work in the locale.

Along with flexible work assignments, workplaces in the future will stress space compression with alternative office settings. Employees will have moveable desks, with computers, fax, cellular phones and other electronic devices to fulfill job assignments wherever the organization needs them. Virtual space utilization will be designed to maximize productivity while utilizing space for a collaborative work culture (Gallagher, 1998). The focus will be on creating an environment for creativity in research and development rather than on structure or fixed facilities as in the past.

Small companies have historically found it difficult to provide fringe benefits such as health insurance to retain employees. Tannenbaum (1999) reported small companies by teaming up with others are beginning to offer employees health insurance through a bi-monthly, or weekly payroll deduction plan. Other benefit plans include auto insurance, discounted merchandise and financial services through payroll deductions.

Wynter (1999) reported that major corporations including Hewlett-Packard, DuPont, and Eastman Kodak, were promoting a new diversity kit aimed at employees with young children. The kit was the idea of Julie Baskin Brooks, whose seven-year-old son was held by three white schoolmates who held a knife to his throat and told him he was no good because he was burnt. Ms. Brooks son became so depressed after the incident he was put on a suicide watch, and recovered after ten months of intensive therapies. These efforts to encourage and teach tolerance toward other races, genders, disabilities or sexual preferences, and ages, will be increasingly important in the 21st century as the percentage of minorities and culturally different populations become an ever-more important part of the nation's workforce. President William Clinton has initiated several programs to deal with hate language, violence, and intolerance.

Belsie (1998) points to an emerging effort by the nation's major corporations to try to live up to codes of conduct about commitment to the customer and responsibility to employees. The largest corporations have full-time ethics officers enforcing codes and training employees on how to use them. Belsie finds that the ethics movement got a boost in the 1980s after the public learned defense contractors were overcharging the federal government. In the 1990s the government enacted federal ethical guidelines to prevent unethical behavior in pricing and employee actions. In recent years major corporation costs for sexual, racial and age discrimination lawsuits have led to increased attention to language and behavior monitoring of their employees.

Workers currently in senior citizen ranks, retired or still working, had a work life that provided lifetime employment with one company, institution or organization. In the past employees had a feeling of loyalty to their company which was reciprocated with a form of paternalism—health care, retirement benefits, and often part-time employment after retirement. There were always notable exceptions to employer paternalism often leading to unionization, labor strife and strikes. Long term employment led to economic and social stability. In the last few decades with globalization and interdependence, workers have had to adjust to job changing, recycling and retraining to meet demands of emerging markets. Reliance on a sense of job ownership or a stakeholder relationship for long term employment within an organization is passe. The workers of the future will have to acknowledge from their first day on the job that they can be replaced, their jobs may be redefined, eliminated, modified, and savings for health care and/or retirement in the future may be their responsibility.

Corporations frequently change pension benefit policy to a cash-balance plan detrimental to long term employees. Often the employees are not notified of the pension policy change. Schultz (1998) found that employers often fail to inform employees of changed pension policies because workers will be angry if they learn about such a policy. Schultz noted that one twenty-five-year veteran employee stated that it would be nice if the company told people they will work for a number of years without the benefit of improving their pension standing. The employee, not wanting to be identified for fear of being known as a troublemaker, calculated that she had to work seven years before earning new pension benefits. As employees find out about the change in corporate pension plans, companies will give increased attention to communicating pension policy change with workers. Increased litigation in the work force is an offshoot of uncertain and undependable employment. Belsie (1998) noted many corporations are currently increasing their community volunteer efforts, as well as matching employee lay-offs and force reductions with funds to assist and retrain workers who lost their jobs.

Maxon (1998) points to a trend among corporations to strive for a more friendly, kind, humane work culture. American Airline executives are seeking to have more satisfied workers through a variety of measures. Hiring executives with people skills, providing seminars, workshops, to react to employee concerns and interests, moving from grading managers less on numbers than on intangibles about how they respond to employees and customers, are some of the initiatives taken at American Airlines. Herman and Gioia (1998) discuss the importance of corporate social responsibility to make work more meaningful and recognize employees for their contributions to the company and society. They see the vital import of improving the quality of life for employees in order to have a healthy organization. Stead (1998) reviewed Richard Sennett's *The Corrosion of Character* (1998) which identified the down-side of the trend toward flexible workplaces. Sennett found the world of flex time, teams and short term projects in a re-engineered, routine-bashing workplace is as bad or worse than the rigid bureaucracy it is replacing. He continued by noting that workers and managers who have to move constantly from job to job, managers who felt a lack of control due to workers distances from home offices, workers who can only be contacted through e-mail, fragmented busy lives surrounded by cell phones, and hi-tech environments, a culture of uncertainty and a lack of social bonds based on trust because they are encouraged to jump from project to project, may well lead to an unhealthy collegially deprived workforce. Sennett noted a case of a Boston bakery that moved from a traditional work culture to the modern new economy of hi-tech, flex time. Workers at the new economy bakery have computer-supervised baking, determined by the temporary daily needs of their local market niche. Mounts of bagels are made one day, stacks of French bread the next, lead to a disconnected and often frustrated worker.

Van Patten, Stone and Chen (1997) noted that corporations are responding to critics of the unforeseen side effects of capitalism (large employee lay-offs, downsizing, restructuring, mergers) on employees and their families by enlarging their community volunteerism as well as providing for recycling and retraining employees laid off for new jobs in growth fields. Other corporations such as Tyson, Inc. provide for English as a second language program as well as giving employees an opportunity to complete their G.E.D. high school degrees through released time. Under pressure to serve the needs of a changing workforce as well as to be good citizens, the business community has been encouraged by President Clinton to be models of corporate responsibility for their communities and nation. The challenge of finding and maintaining humaneness and a sense of common values in an industrialized, global interdependent world remains a concern nearly seventy years after John Dewey articulated the challenge in his 1936 book *Individualism: Old and New* (Van Patten, Stone and Chen, 1997: ix).

Forman (1998) discussed *Legacy Personnel*, a small 12-employee Fort Lauderdale Company, which won an award from the White House last year for running a flexible work environment. The company has a rule that employees must bring their babies to work with them until they are six months old. The walls have artwork, children's facilities for naps are available in the break room. Telecommunication from out of state home offices with periodic company visits whenneeded, led to the family friendly policies recognized by the award from President Clinton in the White House Rose Garden. Although these flexible benefits are not available to the company's 250 temporary workers because they don't come into the main office, there is provision for a corporate discount for these workers at daycare centers. Forman reported that Bureau of Labor Statistics reveal that more than 76 percent of women age 25-34 were in the labor force in 1997 compared to 71 percent in 1986. Six out of every 10 mothers of children younger than 6 are in the workforce. Family friendly policies are good business. Such policies lead to a reduction or even elimination of lateness, absenteeism and worker stress.

Herman and Gioia (1998) found that workers and managers will continue to face new challenges and demands in the fast-moving, unforgiving business climate of the twenty-first century. Survival Herman and Gioia noted will depend on teamwork, loyalty and vision at every level. Meaningful work and rewards will be vital in the future. As I noted earlier, leadership skills will be vital in creating and maintaining a healthy organizational culture. Organizational morale is complex as is individual behavior. Treating individuals with civility and respect while encouraging performance excellence is the challenge of leaders for the new century. Workplace politics is a given but fairness in employee treatment should be a basic tenant of a humanistic organizational culture.

Hunter (1998) president of Collaborative Futures International, reported that organizations and patterns of relationships are being impacted by change drivers and are adapting. Significant patterns of change for the new century include:

Significant patterns of change for the new century

- Globalization and relentless integration.
- Changing nature of work.
- Acceleration of the pace of business and life.
- More complex organizational systems—processes, structures, capabilities and performance.
- Increased discipline and rigor as well as security.
- Greater need for continuous organizational capacity development.
- Increased stratification—gap between those who are keeping up and those who are left behind, globally, nationally, and locally.
- Move toward life-long learning by individuals and organizations.
- Widening understanding that knowledge and the ability to use it are the most valuable assets of organizations. (Hunter, 1998: 21).

Lou Holtz (1998) currently University of South Carolina coach and former Notre Dame and University of Arkansas football coach and noted motivator, found a philosophy of "do right", applies to coaching as well as to life. His three questions might well form a basis for employer-employee relationships across the workforce spectrum:

1) Can I trust you? Each of us in whatever level of our work life needs to feel, believe and know that there is trust between management, colleagues and the worker. Has the person ever lied, taken ethical shortcuts, spoken in "lawyer-ese" or using deliberately vague, misleading, or ambiguous language (Holtz: 201) Few in the workforce have not felt a loss of self-esteem, a feeling of being out of the information loop, a knowledge of being manipulated by shifting power centers, and subtle or overt forms of discrimination due to gender, race, ethnicity, cultural diversity or age. Workers become alienated, isolated, and often reflect emotional and physical illness due to such job-related events. It is not uncommon to have a supervisor approach a new employee and ask for reports of anyone criticizing management or bad-mouthing organizational initiatives. Such information networks leave employees with doubts as to who to trust. Leadership is a precious commodity and requires reciprocity or support from employees as well. Leaders often feel isolated and when promoted from the workforce to management find it hard to communicate with former colleagues on a friendship basis. Informal rumor networks can work to the disadvantage of a healthy organization.

2) Are you committed to excellence? Individuals should give their maximum effort for every task. An individual's behavior gives a guide to reliability, dependability, and responsibility for actions. Is a person a workhorse or a shirker, is the individual the last to arrive at work and the first to leave, does the person blame others when mistakes are made or things go wrong, are points for comparison with fellow workers (Holtz: 201). There should be a life-long striving toward being the best one can be. Fully using talents, abilities, expanding knowledge, and a commitment to obligations and responsibility to self and others is essential for the good life. Employees need to be given opportunities to learn and grow toward professionalism on the

job. Some organizations and schools have developed zero tolerance for disruptive behavior patterns and shoddy workmanship. A story often told in the business community illustrates this point. A company's product was parachutes. Employees were satisfied with a 3-4 percent failure rate. Management then originated the idea of employees using every fourth parachute. It was not long before there was a zero failure rate since employees were laying their own life on the line. Effective management communication of quality production and products throughout the organization and at all levels involve a commitment from the top down and bottom up to active, reflective and responsive listening and reaction to the needs, goals and concerns of workers and of management needs for product excellence.

3) Do you care about me? Lou Holtz's third point stresses the importance of a feeling of being listened to, respected and cared about. Holtz gives questions for leaders to consider by reversing the three main points. Have you given a person a reason to trust you? Have you demonstrated your commitment to excellence for them? Have you shown how much you care about individuals under your supervision (Holtz: 202)? Unhealthy organizations result from workers' failure to network with each other, unwillingness to go that extra mile when needed, and unfortunately when anger and emotion overtake reason, overt or covert industrial sabotage occurs.

In a society with long-term cycles of boom and bust, government programs are essential in providing a social support network. Social security, welfare, health care, disability, children's care, and a multitude of other programs are essential to maintain stability with society. It is important for a humane workplace to examine the organization culture in order to assure a positive climate. This is especially important since individuals spend most of their days in workplaces.

Efforts to create and maintain a healthy organizational culture were continually challenged by record corporate mergers totaling over $1.6 trillion dollars in 1998 as the global economy impacted bottom line performance. Larger corporations were necessary to remain competitive in the global marketplace. The merger mania led to increased employee firing and lay offs in 1999 and 2000. Although the economy was strong enough to increase the number of available positions in growth areas, employee lay offs led to labor morale problems that will require public and private corporate initiatives to expand retraining, recycling, and financial assistance to the downsized labor sector. These initiatives are vital for maintaining a network to protect marginalized peoples (minorities, unemployed, underemployed, aged, culturally diverse, gender) from falling through the cracks of an inadequate social security system.

Emerging Higher Education Delivery Systems

Higher education was in a period of transition in the mid- to late- 1970s with the Watergate scandal leading to a questioning of the nation's social fabric. Editors of *Change Magazine* sought the participation of leaders to write an essay on their perceptions, projections and prescriptions for higher education institutions for the future. The result was a book entitled *The Third Century* published in 1977. Glazer (1977) wrote the introduction which included future projections of 26 prominent American leaders. Selected future projections included:

- An expansion of life-long learning. More adults will need to recycle, retrain and learn new skills to keep up with new trends in technology and society. In an era of enrollment decline, life-long learning can help institutions to maintain, even grow their student body.
- There will be more off campus learning centers to meet client needs.
- Higher education will increasingly serve those of limited financial means, and those who have not had an opportunity for advanced education due to income, race and sex. There will be a need to balance equality with quality in higher education.

- The push for additional resources will be a necessity in the future. As one author, David Riesman noted, it was difficult to justify the University of Illinois maintaining a world class library when Southern Illinois University was letting tenured faculty go due to inadequate funding resources.
- Governmental intervention in college and university affairs will lead to the danger of bureaucratic binding and limitation of educators.
- It will be necessary to find ways to use technology to offer more economical approaches to higher education.

Each of the projections over two decades ago has come true. Higher education institutions have and are moving rapidly into life-long learning programs and courses. More adults are taking courses, often through distance learning and off campus centers. Diversity has become a major goal in American universities, the search for additional funds especially through corporate America is a reality, governmental intervention in university affairs has become a major issue, technology is being used to reduce costs and maintain services. Most major universities, in response to governmental bureaucratic mandates for accountability and performance assessment, have put in place specific performance criteria and implemented post-tenure review to monitor the teaching, research, publication record of senior professors, especially designed to reduce operating costs through eliminating higher paid senior faculty. With a smaller differential between salaries for entry level and senior faculty, administrators are finding few, if any, cost savings in eliminating senior faculty. In some instances senior faculty receive smaller salaries than entry level faculty. An emerging trend in higher education is hiring adjunct and part-time faculty, which in late 1998 totaled almost half of all professors in the country. Community Colleges, together with small state supported colleges, continue to employ more adjunct and part time faculty than other higher education institutions especially major research institutions.

There is a trend for colleges and universities to support and increase diversity in the staff, faculty, administration and student body. Donald M. Stewart (1998), president of the College Board, reported that 1998 college bound students were more racially, and ethically diverse, more eligible for college credit prior to enrollment, and had higher grades than their predecessors. Disparities in academic preparation, test scores, and other factors are growing across subgroups, according to Steward. Steward continued by noting that despite the recent backlash against affirmative action, racial and ethnic minorities continue to see college as the route to a better life and in 1998 minority students were a record one-third of the SAT population and 28 percent of the advanced placement graduates, and more of them are seeking a master's and Ph.D. degree.

Healy (1998) discussed new innovative programs of Rio Salado College in Tempe, Arizona. Located near the University of Phoenix, one of the largest innovative degree delivery systems universities, Rio Salado has been breaking traditions and the status quo. Rio Salado and the University of Phoenix provide new delivery systems. Both institutions are consumer oriented. Rio Salado, a low-cost college, with an enrollment of 24,717, has opened collegiate programs in high schools, pushed for community colleges to offer baccalaureate degrees, and sought to have universities grant credit for vocational courses. Rio is 20 years old. Its 19 full-time faculty have no traditional departments, nor tenure. Classes are offered every other week over the Internet at some 129 locations and conclude after six or seven weeks. Students are offered a beep-a-tutor program, extra help based on student need. Students can submit the same paper for more than one class, to be evaluated for composition and content. A sense of teamwork is encouraged and students encourage each other to continue and not drop out (Healy 1998).

Parker (1998) reported on the growing importance of the Community/Two Year College in preparing the nation's future workforce. Since the Truman Commission Report in 1947 that espoused expanding community colleges to meet the needs of individuals for education beyond the high school level, these low-tuition institutions have served an increasing percentage of higher education enrollment.

Community colleges currently fill a special place for those who want to improve technical skills for better, higher paying jobs. In addition, community colleges are serving college graduates in their efforts to update their workplace skills. Parker notes that one out of 4 students enrolled in a community college has a bachelor's degree or higher. In late 1998 there were some 5.4 million students enrolled in these two-year colleges. Many students are non-credit enrollees seeking special job-skill training. Community colleges are closely integrated with the business community and students often are quickly hired on completion of their skills training. Parker found community colleges alleviate a critical shortage in skilled professionals and by 2000, estimates 80 percent of all new jobs, especially in information technology will require an education beyond high school but not a four-year degree program. Retraining workers is as vital as first-time education. Community colleges, he reported, have an enrollment of 58 percent female, and 42 percent male. These colleges enroll 45 percent of all undergraduates, 37 percent of all white students in higher education; 42 percent of all African-American students in higher education; 55 percent of all Hispanic students in higher education; 40 percent of all Asian/Pacific Islander students in higher education. Average lifetime earnings for a community college graduate are $250,000 more than for a high school graduate (Parker 1998).

Desruisseaux (1998) reported that two–year colleges are enrolling twice as many foreign students as a decade ago, accounting for some 15 percent of all foreign student enrollments in the United States. While foreign student enrollment in all institutions grew by 7 percent from 1993-1997, it grew by 20 percent in Community Colleges. In an era of restricted financing, foreign students who generally pay full fees, relying on personal or family resources to finance their education, are important to higher education institutions. The Department of Commerce has determined that United States higher education is now the country's fifth-largest service-sector. Other countries are beginning to recruit foreign students more effectively than in the past, which may affect such student enrollment in the future. In 1997-1998, according to Desruisseaux over 57.7 percent of foreign students came from Asian countries with Japan and China leading the way.

As elite private colleges face difficulties in recruiting top flight students, due to universities upping the ante to increase the number of merit scholars, these colleges are working to make their campuses more marketable to students and faculty (Sandler, 1998). Harvard, Yale, Columbia Universities and other leading private universities are investing millions of dollars in rebuilding dormitories and academic halls. Sandler reported that Yale and other elite institutions have been putting more money in classroom, and dorm technology as well as in workout machines in health and physical fitness facilities. Many facilities on elite university campuses were in need of repair after years of neglect. In an era of increased competition for the nation's best students, private institutions are working to raise additional funds from alumni and friends to attract students who have more scholarships and rewards from a larger variety of institutions than in the past. Small liberal arts colleges are having an ever-more difficult time in recruiting and retaining merit scholarship students especially when research universities are often offering grants, chancellors scholarships and a variety of other benefits that far exceeds their student financial needs. A new chancellor at the University of Arkansas in Fayetteville, has expanded scholarships in a recruiting effort to bring in the brightest students that formerly were recruited by the nation's elite colleges and universities. In some instances students have large sums over and above tuition, housing, books and other costs for university enrollment. Small elite liberal arts colleges are often hard pressed to meet the inducements offered by larger universities. All higher education institutions are working to expand their endowment base.

College presidents, chancellors and chief executive officers face daunting challenges in leadership for the future. Harvard University provides "basic training" for new college presidents each year. Clayton (1998) reported the basic training includes tips about protecting time for private life in the face of a multitude of demands ranging from fund raising, to concerns of faculty, alumni and state legislators. Trends toward an emphasis on cost cutting, competing for students, donation dollars, and a more active board of trustees, lead to increased leadership stress and burn out. College presidents can no longer dictate to people, and must regularly justify budgets to state legislators and donors. Over 50 to 70 percent of college presidents' time is taken up with the perpetual drive to raise funds for endowments, programs for excellence and facility upkeep and expansion. Clayton continued by noting college presidents need to have support groups and/ or individuals that can be called on for assistance when needed. Without such support the leadership position can be a lonely unfulfilling job. Often faculty need to be informed of the leadership demands to understand their challenges as well as the rationale for salaries four to five times higher than the top salary of professors or distinguished faculty members.

Schaefer (1998) identifies an emerging litigation area in higher education. A philosophy of post-modernism has become a standard in some colleges and universities. Post-modernism in literature, philosophy and education addresses the issues of what is referred to as marginalized peoples. Individuals who historically have not had access to opportunities for upward mobility, who see themselves as oppressed by a European centered culture, are increasingly vocal in higher education institutions. Schaefer (1998) reported on a professor who was hired by the theater department at Arizona State University to establish a nationally recognized actor training program. At the end of his second year Mr. Jared Sakren was warned by the department head that feminists were offended by selections from Shakespeare which Sakren used in his acting classes. The department head stated that Sakren was a good acting teacher, but what he has brought to his job does not match the explicit goals of the department. The department head clarified her post modern perspective by noting that there is a tension between the use of a Euro-American canon of dramatic literature and production style vs. post-modern feminist/ethnic canons and production styles. The department head continued by noting that each of us must be accountable—to students, other areas in the department, to the chair, to the dean—no one in this department is a free agent. Although he had strong student support and endorsement, an admission by the department head that she destroyed positive student evaluations, Sakren had no success appealing his dismissal through university channels. Schaefer concludes his report by noting that Sakren has resorted to a lawsuit charging racial discrimination because of his European descent and his use of works written by male European counterparts.

Gold (1999) reported that the Florida legislature allocated over $40 million in public funds for student vouchers for private higher education institutions for 1998-1999. Private colleges throughout the state are seeking to increase the state program to over $70 million. This program is similar to the public school voucher program.

There are many views of the philosophy of post-modernism. Advocates indicate the importance of examining in detail societal racism, discrimination against peoples of color, women, those with sexual preferences different from the norm, and there is an increasing amount of literature addressing those issues. Opponents of post-modernism debate the issue of scholarship quality and the tendency to deny students access to the literature that has in the past reflected the best ideals of humankind.

Public and Private Education

Cremin (1990) in his *American Education: The Metropolitan Experience* found three abiding characteristics or trends in American Education. The first characteristic was popularization or the tendency to make education widely available in forms that are increasingly accessible to diverse peoples. The second trend Cremin referred to as multitudinousness or the proliferation and multiplication of institutions to provide that wide availability and that increasing accessibility. The third characteristic was politicization or the effort to solve certain social problems indirectly through education instead of directly through politics. Cremin's (1989) *Popular Education and Its Discontents* foresaw a rising chorus of dissatisfaction, especially in regard to academic standards, that has accompanied the popularization of education in the United States since the 19th century. Cremin continued by noting that radical changes in technology including television require a broader approach to education. In the future colleges and schools will not be able to accomplish educational tasks of a post-industrial society on their own. Collaboration among educators, parents, community and business representatives in conjunction with collaboration among many public and private agencies run by many different kinds of professional, most of whom are not in the habit of sharing budgets, facilities, and clientele will need to be involved in education in the future. Cremin continued by noting that opportunities to examine alternatives in values, ideas, aspirations and choice are essential in any education that benefits a free people. These alternatives must not be lost in the effort to enhance efficiency. The perpetual push for innovation, change and stability are part of the participatory process of education in a free society.

State educational reforms reports include a call for more technologically skilled workers to meet corporation employment needs to maintain global competitiveness. Several governors are working on initiatives to assure elementary students are achieving at or above grade achievement levels. Arkansas Governor Mike Huckabee has implemented a K-4 program, SmartStart, to provide mentors, more teachers, and increased funding for elementary schools and teachers. The program is designed to guide students to better elementary school achievement. Ending student automatic promotion in public schools as well as increasing funding for preparing students for higher education institutions are other state education initiatives. Business, community, school collaboration efforts are increasingly utilized to prepare students for a global super-information economy. Business leaders are taking the initiative in articulating employee needs for the 21st century. Parents often contribute time and funds to assist teachers in public schools. Retired individuals are contributing in increasing numbers to a variety of support work in public schools. Many serve as tutors for reading and mathematics assistance. Enlightened school administrators often have special appreciation luncheons for parents, the retired and grandparents. Reaching out to senior citizens, grandparents and other community groups has proven most beneficial in gaining support for bond issues. With an increasing number of immigrants with English as a second language deficiencies, reading and language arts teacher aides are in demand and needed. It has been found that many parents and grandparents with little if any English language abilities, very much want to assist teachers in their tasks. When asked to participate they are eager to take on any task that they are able to do. Such participation gives them a sense of belonging, self-esteem, self-worth and dignity as well as learning English language skills along with their children and grandchildren.

O'Dell (1998) discussed renewed efforts to improve public education through offering warranties certifying the competence of high school graduates. Warranties have been tried in different states in the past with varying degrees of success, but Virginia is considering implementing such a policy. Currently the only other state offering warranties for its public school graduates is Minnesota. Teacher organization officials complain that colleges should be allowed to pass off costs incurred for students they never had to accept. Public schools are required to take any child sent to them. State supported colleges and universities spend over $25 million every year for remedial education in reading, writing, and mathematics. Virginia's Hanover County's public schools provide a warranty for every high school graduate who makes at least a "C" average. O'Dell continued by noting that if a college or employer finds the graduate needs remediation, the school district picks up the cost. Guy (1998) noted that since 1994 Hanover schools have paid only 14 claims averaging about $400 each. Hanover schools represented a wealthy, upscale suburb of Richmond, Virginia. Guy wondered if a warranty program would be viable in South Florida or other parts of the nation with many chronically low-achieving schools and students, overcrowded classrooms, overworked teachers, outdated textbooks and technology, limited language skills in English or in the primary language, and with problematic parental involvement. The challenge facing public school educators in inner cities with large and growing minority populations and in areas with heavy influx of English as a second language students will require persistent and continued efforts to improve student achievement levels.

Although school crime rates are declining, random student violence has been pronounced, adding another dimension to attempts to raise educational standards. Together with crack babies, latchkey children, single parent children, students with AIDS and other diseases, American schools need to take on a caring, supportive, parenting role for children, in addition to creating and maintaining an environment conducive for learning. Although in an ideal society, these challenges would be met by parents and/or primary caregivers, in the real world of the public schools, school-teachers, administrators and staff are asked and required to serve as a universal panacea for societal challenges. If schools did not meet this essential role, who would be able to do it? Experimental alternative school systems, however developed and defined, would face the same issues and need to respond to them.

Newcomb (1998) finds an increasing number of philanthropists, activists, educators and parents growing impatient with public school performance as well as the pace of school reform. These concerns have resulted in more options for education including charter, magnet, private or parochial schools with tuition paid by tax-funded vouchers, public schools with nontraditional curriculum, school choice, and home schools. Americans tend to prefer increased choices in education and a recent Phi Delta Kappa/ Gallup Poll showed that 48 percent wanted more say in the selection and hiring of teachers, up from 41 percent in 1990. The increased stress on school choice, interest in selection and hiring of teachers may have a conservative agenda. Vocal advocates for ideological purposes may represent a threat to a pluralistic society and the public schools that provide an opportunity for students from all backgrounds, races, ages, gender and cultural diversity to learn about a multicultural mosaic.

Alexander (1998) examined the voucher debate in depth. He found that after a quarter of a century of federal and state voucher systems in higher education, public colleges and universities find themselves shortchanged in funding. Initially Alexander reports, higher education vouchers, in the form of federal direct student aid, were justified as a means to expand educational opportunity and to provide lower-income students with choices to obtain high quality in private colleges. Vouchers were also viewed as a means to support private colleges indirectly with public resources, but currently there are growing disparities in expenditures per student which continue to favor private higher education while lower-income students have limited access to private institutions. Alexander also found that as more voucher funds are shifted from need-based to merit-based there will be further diminished opportunities. Alexander concluded by noting that disparity issues inherent in voucher schemes, indicated that this form of financing will tend to result in greater inequality between public and private school students. He predicted that one can expect voucher plans at lower educational levels will produce only marginal increases in choice for lower-income students while increasing inequalities of revenue between public and private schools. Finally, Alexander reported that the negative effects of inequality produced by vouchers almost certainly outweigh the perceived positive effects of choices promised by vouchers.

Charter Schools—School Choice

Alternative schools have a long history. The district school, the Latin Grammar School, the academy, the consolidated comprehensive high school, public and private schools systems are examples of alternative school concepts. Each movement was an effort to meet the needs of changing societal conditions requiring increased options for educating the nation's youth.

With an increasingly fragmented society, alternative school systems reflect an effort to meet varying parental concerns. These concerns include curriculum content, values, discipline, rejection of consensus aims in education and distrust of educational policies. Questioning of curriculum content has been intense particularly in conservative areas of the country. Intense opposition to teaching methods that focus on socialization, diversity, sexual preferences, and aspects of postmodernism is also reflected in parental call for alternative schools. These concerns differ from those of the corporate elites who launched whole public school reform measures. There is often too little oversight of Charter Schools resulting in financial and delivery failures.

Chaddock notes that George Bush in 1991 called on business leaders to work for public school improvement. They pledged $42 million and Walter Annenberg added another $50 million as part of a $500 million grant to help public education. The goal was to develop new educational designs to help all students meet world class standards in at least five core subjects. New American school designs are currently in use in more than 1,000 schools and 31 states. Chaddock reports that there have been successes, but everyone involved in school reform efforts are beginning to realize the complexity of school cultures and the impossibility of solving complex issues through quick technological fixes.

Bottom line assessment of student achievement, test scores, and reforms suggest meager results. Throwing money at a problem will not resolve it, some are finding. Perceptions of what needs to be done vary. Louis Gerstner, CEO of IBM said we can declare some success, but have a system that is failing our children and resisting change. The mood, he continues, in the business community is not good. It is not going toward the reform of U.S. public education but toward its replacement. The performance of our schools is not any better than when we started in 1991. Chester Finn, a senior fellow at the Hudson Institute, finds two grand strategies—one is systematic reform through a centralized top-down management-style improvement and a competition, diversity and choice strategy. The big national CEOs favor systemic reform while venture capitalists favor choice and competition, but both strategies need to intersect for real change to occur (Chaddock: B 5).

Mellor (1998) found that the June 10, 1997 Wisconsin Supreme Court decision upholding the nation's first school choice program against legal challenge may lead to a wider array of choices for parents and students. The Wisconsin program allows up to 15,000 low–income children to use state funds in private or religious schools. The court upheld school choice programs (1) as long as the program is neutral between religious and secular options and (2) parents direct the funds.

Careilli, Mauro, Kronholz (1998) noted that the Supreme Court on November 9, 1998 denied a review of an appeal of the Wisconsin Supreme Court Decision. By denying appeal, the high court gave no decision and set no national precedent. The issue is sure to be raised in future litigation. The National School Boards Association and Americans United for Separation of Church and State had supported a challenge of the Wisconsin school choice program. As Careilli noted, supporters of school choice programs are sure to see the high courts denial of review as a green light to expand the voucher plans.

Meanwhile Congress is exploring a national voucher program, and legislatures in half the states have considered such programs. Kronholz found that vouchers are central to the Republican education policies at both state and national level. Although their power has been weakened by Democratic gains in congress, some see the high courts refusal to overturn the Wisconsin Court's decision a victory for vouchers. Vouchers are government-issued tickets that allow children to attend any school of their parents' choice, with the government paying part or all of the bill. Wisconsin's Department of Public Instruction said 6,100 children are enrolled in the Milwaukee Parental Choice Program, filling all available seats in the city's 84 participating private schools. But 3,000 of those children had already been attending private schools at their family's expense. Meanwhile, the city's public schools are losing $4,950 for each student who didn't enroll in public schools (Kronholz: 1998 A 2). As Mauro noted, recent Supreme Court rulings have cast doubt on a 1973 decision that struck down a voucher program because public money was used to "subsidize and advance the religious mission of sectarian schools".

Although research results vary, independent studies at Harvard, Princeton, and the University of Texas have shown significant improvement in math and reading scores in voucher-supported schools. The ACLU, the National Education Association, People for the American Way, Americans United for Separation of Church and State and the NAACP plan on appealing the Wisconsin decision to the Supreme Court.

Lynn (1998) finds the Wisconsin Court decision strikes a blow against the separation of church and state and against historical commitment to public schools. He also finds that some $14 million will be diverted from needed programs in public schools. Lynn fears that state dollars may be spent for programs from Louis Farrakhan's Nation of Islam, Neo-Nazi Christian Identity Groups or local fundamentalists churches. Lynn fears government regulation of religion will come with demand for accountability in the use of public funds.

Baldauf (1998) finds the Wisconsin court ruling to be a significant victory for school choice advocates. Parents and politicians pushing for greater choice in the type and quality of schools, have led some legal scholars to find that vouchers violate the First Amendment's separation of church and state concept. Other court cases are pending in Vermont, Pennsylvania, Arizona, Maine and Ohio. Shlaes (1998) points out that school choice is not a new idea; academies were formed by New England educators and philanthropists in the early 1800s. When public schools emerged, rural town leaders saw no need to repeat their work and set up a voucher arrangement with the academies called "tuitioning out". St. Johnsbury in Vermont is an example of such an academy with a 10-1 teacher-student ration, 1,000 resumes from teacher candidates, a tuition of $7,090 dollars lower than public school costs per student, a vocational program, serving handicapped and special education students, students performing at the 90 percentile on Advanced Placement tests for English, European and American History, and biology, a larger percentage of the student body going to college than any public high school in the state. School vouchers and choice have a long and often unknown history. St. Johnsbury serves and responds to community needs for facility use as well as for new courses to serve local business and industry needs (Shlaes 1998).

Overview of Charter Schools

Wood (1998) explores an Arizona Charter School, one of 783 others across the United States. The Center for Excellence Charter High School in Phoenix has no lunch room, gymnasium, or library. For reports, students use a bookmobile that parks blocks away. For an occasional art class, they walk to a nearby elementary school. There is one teacher for every 15 students working in carpeted, quiet rooms.

There are no electives but there is an environment that makes it impossible to escape learning. Concentration is on English, math, social studies and science. Wood finds Arizona to be a laboratory for charter schools since their origination in 1994. Supporters cite reduced bureaucracy, restoration of local control, and empowerment of teachers, while detractors cite problems of accountability, questionable standards, elitism and even segregationism. Both supporters and detractors find that Charter Schools have broken the public school monopoly. Some Arizona Charter Schools have been shut down due to various abuses, but the Hudson Institute and the Educational Excellence Network found that Charter Schools may be the most vibrant force in American education today.

Walters (1997) author of *Charter Schools: Creating Hope and Opportunity For American Education* finds such schools challenge the existing power structure. Charter Schools also tap into American values such as opportunity, choice and responsibility. In addition Charter Schools are more appealing than vouchers for private schools. While magnet schools have admissions tests and spend more money per student than other public schools, Charter Schools are not allowed to have admission tests and spend exactly the same per pupil as other public schools.

Charter Schools—Litigation

Charter Schools, like all other school systems in our country, are not immune from litigation, a growing problem for educators. Seligman (1998) pinpoints the challenge of proliferation of lawsuits for educators. He provides several examples of current lawsuits that divert funds needed for education. In 1995, Texas adopted a Robin Hood plan which had the legislature providing make-up funds to school districts with below-average resources. Every year since 1995 the plan's adequacy has been challenged, and a report in the *Bond Buyer* indicates the Texas comptroller is now talking of a need for another $8-$9 billion to equalize standards. New Jersey had three major lawsuits challenging its equalization formula. One of the suits has been brought by a coalition of middle-class school districts claiming that the formula is forcing them to raise property taxes to levels far above the state average. New York and Vermont are facing lawsuits dealing with spending disparity.

Vermont's plan to shift educational resources from richer to poorer districts is under litigation from poor families who live in rich districts, for it offers major tax breaks to rich families in poor districts. Seligman notes the 35-year-old Coleman report's conclusion that educational outcomes or what kids actually learn are decisively affected by family background and only marginally affected by spending on schools. Seligman finds further proof of the validity of Coleman's findings in an article (March 1998) in *The Economic Policy Review* by Eric A. Hanushek of the University of Rochester. Pointing to increased spending and little increase in student achievement, Hanushek says:

> There is little reason to be confident that simply adding more resources to schools as currently constituted will yield performance gains among students.

Charter schools will not be left out of our lawsuit mania. Fister v. Minnesota New Country School (8th Circuit, 1998) suggests additional costs in the future for Charter Schools. In this case 12-year-old Mary Fister solicited information from classmates to supplement her Internet project focusing on deformed frogs. Subsequently one of the parents of a student who provided Mary a quote, sent a letter to Mary asking that her daughter's quote be removed. Mary posted this letter near her desk near a sign that read "Making a Mountain Out of a Molehill". School officials ordered her to remove the letter, but Mary kept putting it back up. She was suspended twice for this behavior and eventually expelled for one year. The District Court's finding that there was no violation of Mary's Constitutional right to free speech nor was it a violation of an equal protection claim since there was no evidence Mary was treated differently from other students. These lawsuits come with a cost to the school and will be a financial challenge into the foreseeable future. Charter schools will surely face increased bureaucracy due to these lawsuits and thus lose one of their rationales for existence.

Charter School Positives

The following information is based on an article by Mulholland and Bierlein (1997). They report that Charter Schools integrate reform movements and develop highly autonomous and accountable learning environments. Educators are forced to question conventional management and instructional practices. Organizers may be teachers, parents, or others from the public or private sector, and sponsors may be local school boards, state education boards or some other public authority. Each school charter includes instructional plans, specific educational results and their measurement, as well as management and financial plans.

Charter Schools Ideally

Enhance educational options
Encourage true decentralization
Focus on results, not inputs
Remain public schools
Offer new professional opportunities for teachers
Foster a more market-driven educational system

Charter School Research on School District Impact

Rofes (1998) conducted a study of Charter Schools' impact on school districts in eight states and the District of Colombia and included case studies of 25 school districts affected by Charter Schools. The study conducted in 1997 and published in a 1998 report *How Are School Districts Responding to Charter Laws and Charter Schools,* included the following findings of their impact on school districts.

- School districts lost students and financing. They lost a particular kind of student to niche-focused charter schools. There was the departure of a significant number of disgruntled parents with shifts in staff morale as well as the redistribution of some central office administrators' time and increased difficulty in predicting student enrollment and planning grade-level placement.
- Of the 25 case-study districts, almost half experienced either strong or moderate impact from charter schools and slightly more than half had experienced either no impact or mild impact. Large urban districts had experienced significantly less impact from charters than rural, suburban and small urban districts.

School District Response to Charter Schools

- The majority of districts carried on business as usual but some 24% significantly altered their educational programs.
- Few superintendents, principals, and teachers in district schools were thinking of charter schools as educational laboratories or were attempting to transfer pedagogical innovations from charters to district schools.
- Charter schools and laws may have contributed to statewide reform efforts that had no formal connection to charters, such as new systems of school accountability, drives for site-based management, and changes in school financing practices (p.1-2).

Whether Charter Schools fade away in the future as other educational innovations and experiments have in the past remains to be seen. Charter Schools have provided a historical continuity for alternative schools.

Charter Schools Summary

Public schools in a pluralistic society based on consensus require a commitment to universal free education for all of the nation's youth. John Dewey called for continued reconstruction of experience through public schooling. He saw schools as a reflection of the larger society facing the same kind of struggles, issues and challenges. George C. Stone (1997) finds in Dewey's theory of community the central purpose of education. This purpose is not just individual growth but for individuals to learn that each of us belongs to many communities and that we move from one community to another during any given day. Each person must learn that he or she has an obligation as a responsible citizen in a democratic social order to act ethically as we move from one community to another. By acting ethically we continually build the great community.

Charter Schools may be seen as attempts to build a great community through alternative routes to learning. They may also be seen as the result of a concerted effort to implement an industrial/business approach to learning and education. Conservative groups have varying agendas to deal with perceived failings in public schools including emphasis on diversity, sexual preferences, third world post-modern orientation, sex education, gender issues, and value education. As

Thorstein Veblen noted at the turn of the century, "education apes business" (Van Patten and Fisher 1997).

Public schools face challenges not of their own making. The *Imperfect Panacea* notes that the public schools have been asked to solve all manner of religious, social, national, and even intellectual problems. Public schools have been lightning rods for discontented critics of the right and left of the political spectrum. Litigation has influenced educational policy and led to increased costs for education. Universities have been seeking to build status through increasing the amounts of grants. Faculty members frequently use public schools as a research laboratory for grant acquisition and implementation requiring increased teacher time on tasks other than teaching. Central public school administrators frequently seek to implement the latest fad in the field placing additional burdens on teachers and staff.

Currently some elementary school teachers have to start the new year using three different methods of reading instruction; they were required to attend a variety of workshops three to four days before faculty planning days, unpaid, and on their own vacation time. First grade teachers are required to use the latest technology including computers in instruction as well as dealing with the latest state education department bureaucratic mandates. Several state education departments are seeking to reduce the number of rules, and regulations to give teachers more time for preparation and teaching.

Criticism of public schools can be found throughout our educational history. "Soap and schooling are not as sudden as a massacre, but are more deadly in the long run," said Mark Twain. His opinion of schooling is matched by Margaret Mead's, "My Grandmother wanted me to get an education, so she kept me out of school," and Ralph Waldo Emerson's response to Horace Mann's lecture in 1839 crusading for the public school. Emerson said: "We are shut in schools for ten or fifteen years, and come out at last with a bellyful of words and do not know a thing." (Gross, 1975). Vouchers and Charter Schools are the result of increased public school criticism. Both vouchers and charter schools are viewed by their supporters as routes to breaking what is seen as public school monopolies.

As of February 17, 1999, there were some 34 state charter school laws in the United States, with over 166,000 students in 26 states and the District of Colombia. Charter School states with strong to medium strength laws include Arizona, California, Colorado, Connecticut,

Delaware, District of Columbia, Florida, Illinois, Louisiana, Massachusetts, Michigan, Minnesota, Missouri, New Hampshire, New Jersey, North Carolina, Ohio, Pennsylvania, South Carolina, Texas, Utah, Wisconsin. Those states that have weak charter school laws include Alaska, Arkansas, Georgia, Hawaii, Idaho, Kansas, Mississippi, Nevada, New Mexico, Rhode Island, Virginia, and Wyoming (1998, The Center for Education Reform). There are over 1,100 charter schools in operation. President Clinton is calling for 3,000 charter schools by 2,002.

Elder, Jr. (1998) reported that the Texas Legislature like others throughout the nation plans to expand the Charter School program with the Texas Education Agency estimating by 2000 an increased enrollment from the present 12,000 to 38,000 students with the number of Charter Schools increasing from the current 60 to 150.

Meanwhile some Charter Schools have run into trouble overestimating enrollment and receiving overpayment ranging into the millions of dollars. Elder noted that Texas is considering a former fundamentalist preacher's plan for 30 Charter Schools in the state. The State Board of Education may approve the plan feeling that faith-based programs might reach troubled students where other approaches have failed.

Alternative schools may continue to be a wave of the future under the philosophy of expanded choices for parents and students, until their effectiveness can be more fully assessed. Distance learning programs may provide other avenues for teaching, and learning that will require rethinking traditional education delivery systems and retraining for future outreach technologies. Distance learning outreach programs in some states need improved telephone access and reliability and are in the developmental process. School districts often lack necessary funds for modern equipment for compressed video delivery systems.

Charter Schools may be a worthwhile experimentation to get away from bureaucratic rules and regulations but the influence of a business community determined to implement competition in schooling leads one to question the viability of Charter schools over time. The business community's ruthlessness is seen everyday in the mergers, restructuring, downsizing, and laying off of thousands of people. Organizational loyalty to and concern for long-time dedicated workers is a thing of the past. In turn employees' loyalty to their organization is lessened. Charter Schools, however, represent a strength in that they are public schools oriented toward serving young people regardless of economic, cultural or ethnic backgrounds. Universities are starting to sponsor Charter Schools. Central Missouri State University in Warrensburg is building a number of partnerships with them. Charter schools will face increased scrutiny as they become more prevalent on the American educational landscape. Public school teachers may be eager to teach in charter schools with less bureaucracy after having faced an ever-growing and incessant level of rules, regulations, mandates in their curriculum that are often untried and untested programs and innovations. These factors are often designed, disseminated and implemented with little if any input by teachers whose support is needed if they are to be successful in practice.

Kronholz (1999) reported that there were signs that school competition is beginning to affect public schools. She referred to a study by Eric Rofes, a University of California Researcher who analyzed 25 school districts for signs of competition and found that a quarter of them made big changes to their programs because of Charter Schools. Kronholz found, as others, that early results of Charter School performance are mixed, and outcomes are not always the ones intended.

Future Issues: Public and Private Schools

Simpson (1998) raised questions about forcing public schools to compete with a variety of alternative schools systems. He wondered why sending more children and their tax money to private schools would improve education. Simpson found there is a basic public misconception that public school teachers, staff and administrators are not doing a good job but threatened with economic reprisal, the educrats will deliver more effective student achievement. However Simpson and those of us who have spent a lifetime working with public school teachers know that they are giving their all on behalf of student achievement. Working long hours, getting emotionally drained from trying to get students motivated, involved, and guided to make right choices in learning and living, spending their own money on needed student supplies, attending meetings, contacting parents, attending teacher training conferences and taking night courses to enhance their professional development, are part of the teacher' work life. Often new teachers go home exhausted after school, crying themselves to sleep with concern over the plight of many of their students-at-risk. Some research studies found no noticeable difference in achievement levels of Charter School children together with a focus on financial not student learning. In addition school district administrators are hesitant to adequately supervise Charter Schools. Supporters of Charter Schools believe research reports that find little if any difference in student achievement, overlook the fact that over 2,000 Charter Schools are less than two years old and have not been in business long enough for an accurate appraisal of their effectiveness.

Desegregation of schools through busing students for racial balance has been implemented in the past. Hendrie (1998) found that a growing number of formerly segregated school districts are being freed from court supervision that require busing for racial balance. Hendrie reported that four decades after federal troops were called on to help Little Rock, Arkansas schools, school administrators do not have to assign students to schools across town except to prevent a school from becoming more than 80 percent white. A federal judge's revised plan relieves the Little Rock School District from having to recruit students to obtain a specific racial balance in every school. Double incentive magnet schools will continue to serve neighborhoods with a majority of black students. These magnet schools will receive twice the amount of money as other schools to address issues of social justice. The question remains whether Charter Schools, vouchers, private schools will indeed face the same challenges that public schools do in raising student achievement levels and meeting essential societal goals.

Public schools have to serve all students regardless of motivation, interest, parental involvement, and who are not required to do anything for the privilege of returning each day. Simpson found that if public schools are going to be required to compete with alternative schools systems, then fundamental fairness requires that everyone compete by the same rules. Public schools have to accept anyone who walks in the door but if given the power to hold students to a strict standard of daily accountability, teachers and their schools will be competitive and competent, according to Simpson. Although efforts to pay school districts more money for student achievement improvement have been unsuccessful in the past, Arkansas has proposed rewarding schools with cash for student test score improvement. Under the Arkansas proposal for implementation by 2002, student Stanford test scores in the fifth, seventh and tenth grades and on the state's benchmark exams will provide a base for distribution of funds. Schools would get 0 to 10 points for the percentage of their students who score at or above "proficient" levels on math, reading and language arts tests sections. Arkansas schools and districts failing to meet improvement goals would be classified as "academically distressed" and eventually be taken over by the state if they fail to meet state guidelines. The plan is to be phased in starting in 1999 and will be in full swing by 2002. State education school improvement plans like that of Arkansas, although well intended, often end in increased bureaucracy. Teachers and staff were faced with the added burden of state department rules and regulations that increased the amount of paperwork and decreased the amount of time for instruction. In the past, when funds were to be given to schools for student improvement, students complained that if they were the ones improving, funds should be given to them and the plans were tabled.

On a personal note, I have seen the deep care and compassion teachers have for their students who get involved in non-productive behavior. Sleepless nights, stress, emotionally draining experiences are part of public teachers' work and home life. Often teachers purchase needed supplies for students out of their own paychecks. Many of those who advocate, and stipulate initiatives for school reform, have little understanding of the real world of the public schools. Often teachers who work very hard to motivate, stimulate, and encourage students to learn through innovative and experimental methods, that they have learned through required workshops, seminars, and state mandated programs, find that parental lawsuits challenge their expertise, methodology, values and even student assessments.

Although some demographic researchers predict teacher shortages in the future due to the wave of baby boom offspring entering schools, there may be opportunities to employ well trained and educated retirees to fill the void. Cross (1999), president of the Council of Basic Education, reported that if governmental leaders would remove social security income caps, senior teachers would be attracted by opportunities to return to the classroom, and retirees from other fields could be provided opportunities to retrain for the education profession. Cross concluded by noting that beyond any dollar-and-cents benefits would be the good that would come from connecting our eldest generation to our youngest. As a nation, he continued, we can only benefit by doing more to bring closer those with the wisdom and skills born of age to those who have barely begun life's journey.

Edwards (1998) illustrated the complexity of issues and controversies facing teachers now and in the 21st century. Teachers are increasingly sued or fired or resign in frustration for using books parents find offensive. Teachers use outdated or bland books in order not to offend any ideologically focused group. Even famous classics such as *Catcher in the Rye* or *the Grapes of Wrath* are frequently the object of parental protests. Edwards found that teachers often lack adequate library facilities, and stress anthologies of excerpts or drill on paragraphs to prepare students for state mandated tests. Due to parental protests, some schools now require parental consent forms before the use of any potentially controversial book. Edwards noted that in many cases protesting individuals and groups have not even read the books they are challenging.

Teachers face the challenge of crack babies, as well as social issues including the fact that there are about 1 million teenagers in the United States, some 10 percent of all 15-19 year old women, who become pregnant, according to Maynard (1997). Thirteen percent of these pregnancies are unintended. The United States teen-age pregnancy rate is twice as high as any other advanced industrial nation. A third of these teens abort, 14 percent miscarry, 52 percent or some half a million teens bear children, 72 percent out of wedlock. Maynard continued by noting that teen pregnancy occurs together with poverty and welfare. Other studies have shown teen pregnancies result in more birth defects, health care problems, and costly medical care.

For all of the challenges of our public schools, educators whose schools are seen as a universal panacea for all of society's social ills, there are continuing efforts at the federal and local levels to improve instruction and raise standards. With Congressional gridlock stymieing the President's educational initiatives, the nation's governors, according to Kronholz (1998) are taking the lead in setting national goals. Although polls showed parents in favor of Clinton's proposals for national education tests, conservative Republicans feared federal involvement in education while liberal Democrats feared minorities would fare poorly. Congress, although authorizing the Department of Education to continue writing the tests, provided no funds for the project. According to Kronholz, the nation's governors are including a set of common questions into their state assessments, a technique called embedding. A corporate supported organization, *Achieve*, created to provide support for teachers, administrators and school staffs, was asked by Governors to assist in developing a national embedded test. The need for students prepared for a global economy was an incentive for moving toward uniform standards across state lines, according to Kronholz. Apple (1996) addressed the issue of the nation's at-risk student population by noting that soci-economic relations and structures that organize society play an important role in student achievement as well as economic equity and fairness. In the long run schools and educators must deal with the issue of economic and social justice with equality of opportunity for all of its young people. Educators in the next century will continue to grapple with inner city communities where disadvantaged youth and citizens face boundaries of crime, unemployment, underemployment and a sense of alienation. Developing and involving partnerships, cooperative initiatives among and between parents, guardians, teachers, youth, the corporate sector, the religious community, to develop a community of democratic values will be essential in attacking economic, political and social inequities in the future.

It may be worthwhile remembering Henry Steele Commager's evaluation of American Education that no other people ever demanded so much of education and none other was ever served as well by its schools and educators (Pierce, 1975).

Reinventing and Creating More Responsive, Efficient Government

Feeney (1998) discusses Vice President Gore's vision of making Dallas and Fort Worth a "hassle free zone". Gore and project participants envision an RV going to a local senior center full of people, who on the spot, could untangle Social Security problems, review property tax issues, register citizens to vote and sell transportation passes. Gore's other futuristic visions include citizens going to the local post office on a 24 hour basis and acquiring Internal Revenue Forms through computers. The hassle free community project has no budget and depends on collaboration and interagency networking to provide personnel to solve citizens problems quickly. Eliminating bureaucracy will be a goal of the new initiative for responsive governmental agencies. Cross-cooperation among the various governmental agencies has created intense enthusiasm with participants excited about the potential of reinventing government.

Global Interdependence-Multiculturalism

Illustrations of American provincialism:

> **On Israel**
> - The Arabs and the Jews should settle this problem in a true Christian spirit.
>
>   Warren Austin (U.S. Delegate to the United Nations)
>   offering a solution to the Israel crisis, 1948.
>
> **On Africa**
> - When those countries have a man to lunch, they really have him to lunch.
>
>   Ronald Reagan, (Republican candidate for Governor of
>   California), discussing the emerging African Nations
>   1966.
>
> **On China**
> - We will lift Shanghai up and up, ever up, until it is just like Kansas City.
>
>   Kenneth Wherry (U.S. Senator from Nebraska), 1940.
>   (From Cerf and Navasky: 161-162.

One of the most unfortunate aspects of modern society is the increasing tendency to see problems solely in immediate terms...The majority of the great issues that confront mankind are profound, complex, and, above all, long-term problems. They cannot be resolved swiftly or dramatically; they are closely interrelated; and they bear directly upon the lives of all. For the great problems are global problems, and they require a concerted global approach. It is this fact of global interdependence which is the dominate reality of our time, and will be increasingly so over the next 50 years. The future depends on a system that balances the rights, interests, and aspirations of all peoples.

Kurt Waldheim, 1974

The United States for the first time in its history is a debtor nation often carrying other economies through an imbalance of trade. Capitalism requires global markets to maintain its productive capacity. In a cyclical economy, it is important to develop international financial monitoring of capital flow. Few legislators remember the Smoot-Hawley Tariff acts which led to a worldwide war of rising tariff's and was a factor in a worldwide depression. Cox (1999) found that international trade flow can easily be disrupted. Currently the World Trade Organization is being asked by the American government to retaliate against the European Union for a banana-import system that may violate the organization rules. Although the conflict may be resolved through diplomatic efforts, the danger of disruption of free trade is always a threat to world financial stability.

Capitalism itself is often examined by government officials and scholars in light of perceived harshness of market forces on employment and standards of living particularly for a nation's poorest. Higgins (1999) wrote about Egyptian President Hosni Mubarak's concerns regarding free-market approaches. President Mubarak found the free market approach has failed to help the world's poor and should be rethought. Mubarak spoke to 1600 prominent political, commercial and other leading figures. He noted that in the emerging world there is bitter sentiment of injustice, a sense that there must be something wrong with a system that wipes out years of hard-won development because of market changes. Labor leaders and other groups, attending the international meeting in Davos, Switzerland, suggested free-market approaches has resulted in exclusion, poverty and misery for an ever-increasing number of peoples in emerging and have not nations. There is an urgent need to assist people in need throughout the world. In most countries including the United States, there appears to be a permanent underclass developing that requires intervention programs to assure a decent standard of living for all peoples. There are no easy answers to the challenge of poverty and misery, but international efforts to ameliorate hardships will be a start in the right direction. The United Nations, other world organizations, and private sector efforts on behalf of the poor exist and need to be strengthened for the future. Meanwhile, third world nations need to monitor their financial resources to avoid mismanagement. International speculators in a free world market may destabilize financial markets event threatened nation's currency stability.

The crisis in Asia, Russia and South America represent a challenge to global financial stability. Beyond the political rhetoric so often heard in Congress about buy American, is the essential fact that over 30% of all American jobs are based on foreign investment and trade. Raytheon will cut costs by slashing 16% of its workforce by the end of 1999 due to global financial meltdowns in 1998, according to Meyers (1998). Meyers notes that Merrill Lynch, the financial powerhouse, will fire up to 5% of its traders, Gillette will cut jobs globally and close more than two dozen warehouses and factories, Hewlett-Packard is seeking voluntary buyouts for 2% of its workforce. Auerbach and Pereira (1998) report downsizing and employee reduction by Ziff-Davis, publishers of computer trade magazines. Mc Geehan (1998) notes that up and down Wall Street, employees are bracing for lay-offs. Bankers Trust and Citigroup are planning to cut thousands of jobs. The mood on Wall Street is gray, miserable and filled with employee fear of being jobless. Hemlock (1998) reported that the global financial crisis in Asia and Russia hit Florida's exports hard. While imports rose by 15-17 percent, Florida's exports slumped from 14 percent in 1997 to 8.4 percent through July of 1998. These employment reductions and shifts in trade balance, illustrate now as in the past the cyclical nature of capitalism at home and abroad.

As Maxine Greene (1996) once noted, conservative critics of welfare systems often criticize a single mother of four for getting welfare and not working, while corporations chief executive officers making $20 million a year lay off thousands of workers in the cause of bottom-line results. Foreign governmental leaders seek to balance excesses of free enterprise with necessary social networks for its citizens in need. Weisbrot (1999) pointed to a downside to global capitalism. Financial experts have found that hot money sloshing around the globe can lead to a financial meltdown as occurred last year in Asia when $1,000 billion dollars stampeded for the exit. Buying and selling currency can have detrimental effects in the world economy since the goal of financiers is profit not social stability.

Although there are different viewpoints about the role and function of globalism, Weisbrot (1999) reported that the global economy has no safety net for the poor, no central bank to act as a lender of last resort, no laws or institutions to protect labor or the environment and various world trade organizations may have increased instability and inequality. Weisbrot noted that the promised benefits of freer trade and overseas production, in the form of cheaper consumer goods, have for most Americans been overwhelmed by the downward pressure on their income and the majority of Indonesians now earn less than what they need to buy a subsistence amount of rice. As noted before, some of these challenges are due more to inadequate, out of date, and irresponsible governmental leadership and management than to any economic globalization factors.

Francis (1998) noted that the global outreach of capitalism has become triumphant. She traced the evolution of free enterprise from the robber barons who flourished in the first decade of the 1900s. Their monopolies were destroyed or reduced by anti-trust laws. It is interesting to see how time changes perceptions. John D. Rockefeller's Standard Oil was broken up as a monopoly in restraint of trade by the Supreme Court in 1911. Two of the biggest pieces of Rockefeller's empire were Standard Oil of New York and Standard Oil of New Jersey. Now called Exxon and Mobile, a proposed merger would create one of the world's largest integrated oil companies. In the fall of 1998, market changes led to a merger between two oil giants. The merger demonstrated the ebb and flow of future trends. In 1911, Standard Oil controlled a major share of the world's oil markets demonstrating that history repeats itself, although the percentage of market control was much larger in the past.

Exxon and Mobile combined would control 22 percent of the U.S. retail market (Valdmanis, 1998). Global market competitiveness has led to massive mergers between U.S. corporations as a form of survival in an era of change and market uncertainty. Scherer (1998) found that ten super corporations now have annual revenues of more than $102 billion, larger than the annual gross domestic product of Greece or Finland. The Exxon Mobile merger with $203 billion in revenues makes the corporation equivalent to the 20th largest nation in the world. The mega-firm movement raised some important long-term challenges. Super corporations make it difficult for smaller companies to exist without merging or going into bankruptcy. An advantage for larger corporations is easier access to capital essential in a highly competitive global economy. Scherer concludes by noting that super corporations may not be good for job creation since major worker cutbacks occur on completion of mergers. Large corporations are more difficult to regulate, especially with their global outreach.

Guided and controlled capitalism, making it more humane, has led to creation of wealth and jobs. Child labor laws, job safety, fewer work hours, and improved wages were the result of government laws, rules and regulations, often the result of Labor Unions. Francis noted that the great depression of the 1930s led to more humane labor laws including social security, unemployment insurance, disability payments and health care benefits. Although the United States has had nine recessions since World War II, none have been as serious as the great depression of the 1930s due in part to the creation of the Federal Reserve in 1913. The Federal Reserve manages the flow of money to keep the economy productive as witness Alan Greenspan's recent 1998 decisions to reduce interest rates twice to preserve economic growth and prosperity. Francis continued by noting that controlled capitalism has been an impetus for industrial innovation. The expansion of capitalism throughout the world is a testament to its relevance for the 21st century, although each nation will modify the economic system to meet its own unique and particular needs.

Kodak cameras, mass produced automobiles, provision for transportation systems for increased mobility, telecommunications from the phonograph to radio to television to computers to interactive communication networks of the future, were all the result of giving business and industry opportunities to innovate. "Cultural invasion" from the West is a concern particularly in fundamentalist or closed societies. Peterson (1999) noted that while Barbie with her curvaceous body, miniskirts and platinum blond hair is a big hit with Iranian girls, Iranian officials are rushing to turn out an acceptable Islamic answer to Barbie for the 20th anniversary of the revolution. Their Iranian Sara and Dara dolls with have an "eastern look" with brown hair and brown eyes, and Sara wears a removable head covering called a "hijab" that shows only her face. Peterson continued by noting thatMajid Qaderi, a director at the Institute of Children and Young Adults Developmental Center in Tehran believes that the children of the world all belong to one nation, but the authorities in each country are responsible for those in their own society. Despite warnings from Iranian extremists about the plots hatched by the 'Great Satan', Iranian President Mohamad Khatami believes Iran can learn from and find good in Western Civilization.

Globalization of capitalism is the wave of the future. Currently, according to Francis, there are more than 50,000 'transnational' firms with over 450,000 foreign affiliates spreading modernization as well as producing goods and services. Companies have made over $400 billion of direct investment in plants, equipment, and offices in nations outside those where they were based in 1997. In 1999, 11 European nations introduced a common currency, the euro. Regional trade areas such as the European Common Market will emerge and the challenge for the future is to assure control of tariffs and other trade barriers like the Smoot-Hawley tariffs of the 1930s which might lead to another world wide depression. With the 21st century on our doorstep, and an Asian economic downturn leading to increased job layoffs, there are increasing requests for raising tariffs to protect U.S. businesses and jobs.

Lublin (1998) reported on multinational corporations developing multinational families. With more U.S. companies hiring foreign born managers, and moving them around the globe, executives often end up with families spread throughout the globe, straining budgets and family bonds. Lubin noted that a recent survey revealed a record 67 percent of 177 largely U.S. based companies reported an increase of expatriates who aren't U.S. citizens in their workforce. Eighty one percent of U.S. corporations foresaw growth in their expatriate population by 2000. As corporation's global outreach expands, internationalism in society and families will enrich our understanding of the importance of under-standing and supporting diversity, and multiculturalism in our society.

Although annual stockholders reports are basically promotional materials, a brief overview of a few corporations demonstrate the globalization of our nation's corporate outreach. A sampling of U.S. 1998 businesses reports illustrates the wide scope of globalization. Louis V. Gerstner (1999) C.E.O. of IBM reported global services have grown from $4 billion to $24 billion in just eight years. In the networked society and economy, IBM is modeling pharmacological agents, simulating weather patterns for more accurate forecasting, mining databases in retail or insurance for patterns and insights, seeking solutions in genomics, financial markets, and disease control. Marriott, Jr. (1999), chief executive officer of Marriott International reported on the globalization of Marriott lodging. From one overseas hotel in 1969, 15 in 1989, the global outreach has exploded to 250 international properties with some 67,500 rooms. Meanwhile Marriott continues to be named as being among the best places to work with high employee satisfaction scores. Fisher (1999) C.E.O. of Kodak Corporation is investing over $1 billion in China expanding its historic international presence while moving toward new frontiers in digital products and services. Nye (1999), C.E.O. of Texas Utilities, reported on the globalization of energy production and distribution services to Britain and Australia as energy companies move toward a competitive utilities environment. Armstrong (1999), C.E.O. of ATT reported on the companies continuing effort to move more fully from a domestic company to a global communication power to meet multinational needs for end-to-end quality services.

Third world developing nations continue to face exploding populations although the growth rate is less than in the past. Owens (1998) points to common issues in developing countries. Although Owens was chiefly concerned with Latin America, the same commonalities exist throughout the world of developing nations.

- All are developing at different stages.
- All have a constitutional commitment to free public education.
- All face the challenges that accompany population heterogeneity.
- All have implemented bilingual/intercultural programs.
- All face severe constraints due to few financial resources.
- All see education as a key toward a better future for citizens.

National pride and arrogance continue to challenge global, international interdependence. An absolute conviction that whatever action taken is the right path, with God and truth on their side, the United States military may engage in so-called precision bombing, targeting enemy installations. Unfortunately, such precision bombing may result in what is referred to as 'collateral damage' as innocent civilians near target areas are killed. Manifest Destiny, speak softly and carry a big stick, and the Monroe Doctrine were illustrations of national hubris. Governmental policy makers, using the power of the media to persuade, propagandize and influence public opinion, were able to convince citizens of the universal righteousness of a cause. Failure to understand, sympathize, or listen to the message of other cultures, nations, regions, often results in ineffective, inconsistent, and detrimental foreign policy. "Speak softly and carry a big stick" remains part of the agenda of national policy makers. Intolerance, prejudice, bias, have long been part of American leadership culture. Provincialism wherever it exists creates artificial boundaries, limits the potential of internationalism to improve the condition of humankind throughout the world. Policy makers in the United States who attempt to be dogmatic self-proclaimed beacons of morality and justice throughout the world, are bound to be resented and resisted by other nations. Compromise and diplomacy will be essential for the advance of civilization in the new century. The current military actions in Yugoslavia, may be viewed from many perspectives, but diplomacy and reconstruction of damaged areas are essential in achieving an end scenario.

Isolation, provincialism in our information age can be fatal to corporate survival. German builder, Philipp Hotzmann, AG., discovered the necessity of customer orientation and satisfaction as well as breaking down turf defense barriers. Morais (1999) reported the company almost went under do to lack of coordination among its various operating divisions. In one case the Holzman board turned down a project, but a regional subsidiary went ahead paying more for its raw material, running up loses due in part to lack of communication. French board members did not speak German and German representatives could not speak French. In Global markets, communication is essential. Morais pinpointed the necessity for maximum flexibility and environmental scanning to meet market demands and to diversity the pool of managerial talent. Communication across national boundaries will lead us into a new awareness of the need for an international language for our new century.

Authoritarian regimes are increasingly challenged by new information communication systems. China's officials, for example, are increasingly concerned with the explosive growth of Internetuse which has grown from 100,000 in 1996 to over 5 million today. Platt (1998) found that Beijing is focusing on sophisticated monitoring techniques as well as blocking web sites. China's parliament in 1997 amended the law to forbid electronic messages found to be critical of the government, which can be punished with lengthy imprisonment. Platt reported that Lin Hai who sold some 3,000 e-mail addresses to an online pro-democracy magazine run by Chinese exiles in Washington, D.C. was the first Chinese charged with launching a "cyber" attack on the Communist system. Police ransacked his home, seized his computer and floppy discs. The Internet provides a route for interchange of ideas across boundaries and borders which may threaten existing governmental and social structures, but which at the same time expands global networking and communication across ethnic, national, cultural and racial borders and boundaries. The Internet is a boundary breaker, opening up peoples of the world to new insights, and understandings of one another. An example of this is reported by Walker (1999) who found that in an age of e-mail and fax machines connections among members of a cultural group may be more important than the "vertical" connections within the traditional nation-state. Walker found that Arctic native peoples, the Inuits, some 125,000 strong across Russia, the United States, Canada and Denmark were reaching out to one another across boundaries in times of need. When U.S. and Canadian Inuits learned of hardships of their kin in Russia, they delivered over fourteen tons of foodstuffs to villages in Russian northlands. The Inuits keep in touch through e-mail. Meanwhile, Candada has for the first time in 50 years redrawn its map to create a new territory for the minority population of Inuits with non-natives participating fully in the native government.

By the same token fundamentalism religious or otherwise has led to international terrorism that threatens civilization and social stability. International cooperation to deal with such terrorism is essential since no nation or region is immune from such inhumane acts. President William Clinton sought an increase of $2.8 billion dollars to deal with cyber-era threats. These threats include the use of computers to disable power grids, banking, communication, transportation networks, police, fire, health services, and military assets. Biological attacks such as the nerve gas attacks in the Tokyo subways some four years ago, represent an increasing threat to the world's citizens. Technological advances that can improve lives can also be used to threaten them.

Multiculturalism

As the United States moves from the philosophy of a 'melting pot' where newcomers are assimilated into the mores and folkways of society, to a philosophy of a 'mosaic' or a 'salad bowl' where population diversity is treasured, tolerance of cultural uniqueness becomes more vital. Our diversity is our strength as a nation. President Clinton (1998) put multiculturalism in a larger perspective in his Thanksgiving Day, 1998 proclamation. Excerpts include his tribute to a philosophy of encompassing pluralism in theory and practice:

> We are a Nation of people who have come from many countries, cultures, and creeds. The colonial Thanksgiving at Plymouth in 1621, when

Pilgrims of the Old World mingled in fellowship and celebration with the American Indians of the New World, foreshadowed the challenge and opportunity that such diversity has always offered us: to live together in peace and with respect and appreciation for our differences and to draw on one another's strengths in the work of building a great and Unified Nation.

Molitor (1998) predicted that:

> • Immigration will continue to increase and by 2100, persons of European descent will comprise less that 50% of the population. Hispanics now outnumber African-Americans in 21 U.S. States and will become the largest ethnic minority by 2020.
>
> • Homogeneity will fade as the nation moves toward a mosaic society.

Goodrich (1998) reported that the population of the United States has almost tripled from 92 million in 1910 to over 260 million in the late 1990s. During this period rapid urbanization has taken place with a population shift to the south and west. California, Texas and Florida have gained in population. The electorate has grown more diverse with women and minorities voting in ever-larger numbers. Thousands of women and blacks have been elected to local, state and federal offices nationwide. By 1997, 21 percent of state legislators were women, as well as 22 percent of statewide offices and 11 percent of Congress. Immigration has changed America's population and politics. The open immigration policy that brought millions of Irish and Germans to the U.S. in the mid-19th century brought millions of Italians, East Europeans, and Jews to the nation's largest cities at the beginning of the 20th century.

In the mid-1960s Congress removed ethnic quotas from the immigration policy and there was an influx of Hispanics and Asians creating new voting groups who began working their way into the political system. Goodrich continued by noting although the federal government has grown larger over the years as it provided necessary social networks, political parties found it increasingly difficult to maintain discipline of their members and with no clear mandate for either party, the future promises to be one of intense political struggle. With a fragmented society, sending different messages, the possibility of governmental gridlock needs to be dealt with through attempts at bipartisanship.

Recent arrivals among the foreign born are more likely to live in poverty, have lower incomes, and higher unemployment rates than native born. After being within the country for six or more years their living condition has generally improved. People born in Central, South America or the Caribbean accounted for 52 percent of the total foreign born population with seven million or 27 percent of the foreign born originating in Mexico (1998, Some Facts About the Flow of People Into the U.S.). One can find dual language (English and Spanish) used in most public facilities in the United States.

DelCour (1998) reported that J. Harvie Wilkinson III, Chief Judge of the Fourth Circuit Court of Appeals, asking how will America and its institutions deal with a society rapidly moving into multiracialism— where every American becomes a minority because there is no racial or ethnic majority. As we come to the end of a century, there have been major demographic changes with foreign-born populations increasing and America facing no racial nor ethnic majority by mid-21st century. DelCour notes that there are currently five school districts in the nation that serve more than 100 racial and ethnic groups. Chief Justice John Marshall Harlan once noted that our Constitution is colorblind, and neither knows nor tolerates classes among citizens. This is particularly pertinent currently as we face a future of racial fragmentation if there is overemphasis on affirmative action and under-emphasis on race-neutral policies. There are strong vocal advocates on both sides of the issue.

Voters in California passed Proposition 227, which replaced a dual-language system in which students were taught English but learned other subjects in their native tongue. Critics, including parents, of students receiving bi-lingual education, complained that the system led to high dropout rates and low English literacy. California had recruited some 400 bi-lingual teachers from Spain. These teachers are now in limbo as they try to teach students in English while working hard to learn English themselves (Harrington, 1998). This action in California illustrates the challenges in dealing with multiculturalism in society and in a sense may represent at least partially a return to a melting pot or assimilation philosophy so popular in the early years of the republic. With an influx of new citizens in American society special programs are developed to help newcomers adjust to a different culture.

Baker (1998) reported on a program run by the United Services Organization that serves American military communities. "Brides Schools" caters to hundreds of Korean women who marry American servicemen stationed in Korea and move to the United States. Brides are taught American customs while maintaining a Korean identity. Postnatal care is a difficult concept to grasp. Baker found Korean women believe their *ki*, or energy is depleted during childbirth and spend three weeks in bed eating soup after giving childbirth. It is an adjustment to find American doctors expect more activity after birth. Husbands are taught Korean culture and learn about the bonding of two families after marriage. Such adjustments are part of America's ever-growing population diversity. Communication will be an increasingly vital factor as we become a more multicultural society. Technology will be an important element in the quality of communication in the future. Monitoring of language interpretation will be vital as well.

Bilingualism, English as a second language, and possibilities of language translation through the Internet and computer programming will be vital in transnational communications in the future. Moseley (1999) reported that NATO's recent bombing of a Kosovo Liberation army base was due to a spelling error. While television crews filmed KLA fighters who won a former Serb military base at Kosare, NATO planners misspelled the name on their target maps referring to the base as Kosani. A NATO spokesman blamed the bombing of the Kosovo liberation army base on the spelling error. During the same time, while the British pushed for the use of ground troops in Kosovo, front-page banner headlines in Britain reported that German Chancellor Gerhard Schroeder in a speech called such action unthinkable. Further investigation revealed an Italian interpreter translated the speech incorrectly. The Chancellor used *kimmt nicht* which should have been translated as "ground troops were not being considered" not *undekbar* which referred to "unthinkable". These illustrations point to the importance of correct language translation which can effect international business as well as military actions in an area where many different languages are used.

These are a few examples of social trends as we approach the 21st century. One could provide similar examples of good citizenship, human civility and decency. Habitat for Humanity, volunteer work in civic organizations, in hospitals, libraries and schools all reflect the best practices of citizenship. Yet even these organizations are forced to increase insurance policies to protect themselves from lawsuits. The outreach of civic organizations to all citizens regardless of race, ethnicity, gender, age or cultural diversity, provides the human energy to make their communities better places to live.

Health Care for the 21ˢᵗ Century

Friend (1998) described human embryo cells that have been isolated and grown in a test tube for the first time. The development could lead to new drug therapies and repairing diseased organs in the body. New organs might be grown in the future as well cell transplants to treat disease. The cells grown by James Thompson and others at the University of Wisconsin might lead to opening secrets to human development. The cells in the future might lead to new heart, brain, liver cells with a multitude of possibilities for treating diseases. Nerve cells could be developed and altered to deal with Alzheimer's, diabetes, and Parkinson's disease.

Isaacson (1999) noted that before this century, medicine consisted mainly of amputation saws, morphine and crude remedies that were about as effective as bloodletting. Since then, Isaacson noted, antibiotics and vaccines have vanquished entire classes of diseases. Isaacson found that the next medical revolution will involve genetic engineering which has the potential to conquer cancer, grow new blood vessels in the heart, block the growth of blood vessels in tumors, create new organs from stem cells and potentially even reset the primeval genetic coding that causes cells to age. Our children may be able to choose their kids' traits, select their gender and eye color, tinker with their IQs, personalities, and athletic abilities, clone themselves or others, dead or alive, that they have admired. Isaacson concluded by noting that by the turn of the next century it might be possible to map our genes, the ten billion or more neurons of brains, and create artificial intelligence that thinks and experiences consciousness similar to the human brain as the 20th century's revolution in infotechnology merges with the 21st century's revolution in biotechnology.

Spotts (1998) discussed a major biological breakthrough that is expected to lead to more effective treatment of disease. Drawing material from surplus embryos and aborted fetuses, research teams have isolated and nurtured the basic cell type from which other cells emerge. Spotts believes the new breakthrough may become entangled with Congressional debate over the use of human embryos for biomedical research. Anti-abortionists and certain religious leaders will be against fetal research while doctors and research biologists will support such research that can enrich, enlarge and improve the quality of life for individuals with special health care needs. Long term embryonic stem cells will be stimulated to develop into specific tissue cells for organ and other transplants while short term use of the cells will include genetic studies and drug screening. Spotts concludes by noting that the debate over federal funding for biomedical research will lead to opposition groups that hold that human life begins and remains sacred from conception while supporters will include doctors and medical researchers. Recer (1999) reported that a patient's own cells may be used to grow new organs. These stem cells, the foundation source of the body's tissue may be able to make new skin, liver and other organs. In the future these new discoveries could eliminate the need for utilization of embryos which have been controversial.

There are over 25,000 frozen embryos that are now in clinics in the United States. Their use is being debated and may have to be litigated in the future. Rubin (1998) reported on infertility clinics throughout the country, with leftovers from attempts at in vitro fertilization. In vitro fertilization sperm and egg are mixed in a petri dish with the hope fertilization will occur. While couples debate what to do with the embryos, often paying $1,000 a year for storage, a trend toward arranging for embryo adoption or donation is increasingly common. Single women or couples are increasingly willing to try embryo adoption although there is the problem birth parents will seek to get their babies back after birth. Rubin continued by noting that to alleviate the problem of birth parents seeking return of their child, some agencies offer the opportunity for embryo donors and recipients to meet and get acquainted.

Meanwhile escalating health care costs have led to managed care programs which have been controversial in their attempts to save funds rather than provide needed health care. Often employees with minimal training make health care decisions about which treatments to approve or disapprove for funding. Managed health organizations often have restrictions on geographic areas in which they will pay for needed health care. Individuals who go out of the state in which insurance is issued, often have to pay for their medical bills out of pocket. The trend for managed care is to increase costs to policy holders and decrease services that are offered to patients. In the early and mid 1990's, Hillary Clinton pulled a task force together to deal with national health care especially for the population that was uninsured or unable to pay for needed medical insurance. The political fall-out from health care organizations protests was so powerful, that the effort to improve medical services for the uninsured and nation's poor was terminated.

In early 1999, chief executive officers of health care organizations were seeking to get Congress to implement some of the reforms that Hillary Clinton's task force recommended. These administrators were being seriously challenged to provided needed health care to an increasing portion of the population especially with massive employee layoffs from major corporations. Although there was considerable debate about managed care successes, Jurgensen (1998) found that scores of managed care plans either quit or sharply reduced Medicare coverage with over 444,000 seniors in 30 states forced to select and receive needed, affordable, comprehensive health care in other companies. Managed care officials who promised better health care plans, blamed rising treatment costs, new federal regulations and punishing caps on Medicare reimbursement for the industry's problems. Jurgensen continued by noting that managed care administrators sold power elites on their ability to limit the costs of health care for the elderly and then failed to live up to an adequate care commitment made to them. Congress, according to Jurgensen, has a lot to learn about turning health care over to private managed care organizations. Kahn III (1998) gave another side of the managed care problems. Kahn III, the President of the Health Association of America, stated that the problem could be solved if the government provided more revenues and less expensive regulation.

It is clear that the United States government has to play a larger role in health maintenance for citizens, particularly the elderly and those with inadequate financial resources. U.S. Health Care Officials that oversee the federal Medicare program gathered data on consumer satisfaction and concerns to provide information for senior citizens. Such governmental initiatives were essential since the number of health maintenance organizations dropping insurance for the elderly had increased (Medicare Report, 1998).

Adams and Moss (1998) found nursing homes owned by major health care organizations stressed filling as many beds as possible by residents covered by generous private insurance or Medicare. Adams and Moss noted that patients whose high-paying benefits expired, were to be moved out as soon as possible. The authors found that a nurse in one care home reported her job was to lie, manipulate, and tell half-truths to relatives in order to have them move patients whose benefits had expired. The major health care provider, Vencor, changed its policy and apologized for evicting Medicare patients, but according to Adams and Moss, the company faced the challenge of management turmoil, sinking profits and investigations of its admission and care policies, mirroring challenges of the nursing-home chains nationwide.

Meanwhile Meyer (1998) pointed out that health care costs are rising more sharply than at any time in the past five years. The annual open enrollment time for health insurance options found employees facing increased premium costs and scaled back benefits. Many small employers were considering scaling back or dropping health care coverage completely. Meyer continued by noting that health care corporations continue to try to squeeze costs out of the medical care system. Managed care will be a major political and social issue for the 21st century as employees, the poor, the elderly seek Congressional legislation to meet health care needs, and private health insurance companies seek to maintain and or increase profits.

Search for Civility

Lampman (1998) discusses the work of Stephen Carter on fostering trust and civility. Civility requires that we express ourselves in ways that demonstrate our respect for others as well as recognizing the need to sacrifice for others, including strangers. Carter's book *Civility, Manners, Morals and the Etiquette of Democracy* comes during a time when civility is under attack in our society. Political attacks, abusive language in music, movies and everyday encounters from fist fights on talk shows to road rage, from the sexualization of advertising, to people acting in ways that threaten to isolate us from one another as fear, distrust and alienation occur.

Finding Aristotle's Golden Mean for a sense of balance within society and its governing bodies is increasingly difficult as individually and collectively people move between absolutism, dogmatism and reification of opinions and actions.

There are many forms of hardening of the categories. Individuals fail to listen to one another, often wear a chip on their shoulders, and are unaware of the need for reasoned debate for civilization. Hate crimes together with explosive violence even within our elementary schools, suggest a society under threat to its social fabric.

House Republicans and Democrats plan to repeat a 1997 retreat in Hershey, Pennsylvania. So difficult has it been to find a path to bipartisan governance that Congresspersons have been even planning a get together with family members to find a way to communicate with each other more civilly and humanely. Hershey retreat organizers are planning for 250 participants from the 435 membership of the House of Representatives (Leavitt, 1998). In a fragmented society with members of Congress getting different messages from their constituents, being able to network with each other on behalf of the nation's citizens and responding to their concerns is vital for democracy in theory and practice. Governmental leaders reflect the age in which we live with confrontation, in your face communication, inconsistent with historical civilized behavior. Whether that modus operandi will continue in the future is open to question. As the chapter on the power of the media within society suggests however, civility, compassion, humaneness may well be an illusive goal for the foreseeable future.

Some Reflections on Ethics and the Future

Major corporations employ data gatherers to find out as much as possible about their competition, ways they can save money by gaining information about successes or failures of other companies, and to maintain competitiveness in the global marketplace. Cooper (1998) illustrated this activity. A young blonde, for example, may grab an oil executive for a dance at a Bourbon Street bar. She is not interested in romance but what her dance partner may know about underwater oil acreage in the Gulf of Mexico. As an information gatherer or scout for Murphy Oil, she may find out whether or not it would be worth sinking another oil well in an area being drilled by other oil companies. Cooper noted that all major oil firms rely on scouts to keep up with rivals and to determine cost-effective drilling zones. Cooper related the success of the young blonde scout, a newcomer to the business, with less than 10 years experience. When the dance music ended, the executive "spilled his guts", according to the young single blonde and after depositing the young man on the bar stool, returned to her own light beer with the studied observation "It's always best to get them drunk first".

Cooper reported that some corporations have as many as a dozen scouts, armed with the latest night-vision scopes and cellular phone scanners, operating in an active drilling area. Hymowitz (1998) reported that a 1995 survey of 30 recent Harvard Business School graduates found that most had been pressured by their bosses to do things they felt were sleazy, unethical or illegal. One management trainee was pressured to inflate a return-on-investment figure, while another was told to make up data to support a new-product introduction. "Just do it" he reported his boss told him. Chief administrators set the tone for an organizational culture. Hymowitz found workplace dalliances between bosses and subordinates are so frequent that most companies no longer outlaw them, but simply reassign a new boss to an underling who is romantically attached to a chief administrator within the organization.

DuPont, one of the nation's premier companies, agreed to pay $2.5 million apiece to each of Georgia's four laws schools in a deal to settle charges it withheld evidence during a civil case in 1993. DuPont was sued by a group of nurseries who alleged its fungicide ruined their crops. A Federal U.S. District judge ordered DuPont to pay for a professorial chair devoted to professional ethics in Georgia's law schools (Associated Press, 1998)

Anderson (1998), director of the Social Affairs Unit, a London think tank, bemoans the trend toward work without virtue and the decline of professionalism. Anderson found nursing and patient morale to be in sharp decline. Nurses leaving the profession, dropping out of training courses, not entering the profession, in some hospitals patients being washed while in others, patients are found lying in a bed with food congealing on a nearby plate, but surrounded by the latest diagnostic equipment. Anderson noted the history of silence, obedience, duty, uniforms, formality, discipline and service of looking to the care of patients in the era of Florence Nightingale. In the modern era of rational efficient management, of hot bedding or the rational use of scarce resources to maximize output, and in an era of egalitarianism and individual professional autonomy in which the cult of informality and feminism reign supreme, old fashioned service and virtue are not easily found. Anderson concludes by noting that the late 20th century has tried to have professions without virtue but it has not worked. The era of service, quiet, formality in the nursing and other professions, was about entering a community, a college of others with the same character. Virtue and the ethics of service in an age of a cult of efficiency is sorely needed for a new century. Humanism in our interactions with others needs to be rediscovered.

The Future

Robert Heilbroner proposes to ask whether:

It is imaginable to exercise effective control over the future-shaping forces of today. This rescues us from the impossible attempt to predict the shape of tomorrow, and leaves us with the somewhat less futile effort of inquiring into the possibilities of changing or controlling the trends of the present.

Robert Heilbroner, *Visions of the Future*: 95

Lampman (1998) reported that George Gallup, Jr. believes that while Americans are still intrigued by outer space, they are beginning to focus on inner space as a frontier for the 21st century. Gallup noted that while much has been written about spirituality—the search for meaning in life and for the sacred—it hasn't been the focus of scientific study. He continued by noting that we know little about the profound experiences that are life-transforming for one-third of the populace. Gallup reported that individuals are in a retreat from materialism and are trying to get out of all kinds of bondage: alcohol and drugs, food, narcissism but don't know what they believe and why with some of the spirituality more self-oriented than God-oriented. Individuals are seeking more meaningful relationships through meeting in small groups for discussion and religious study—a silent revolution.

John Dewey's search for the great community reflects an awareness of the challenges to an open society. As our economy is affected by globalization, and our citizenry becomes more diverse, the need for addressing anger, hostility, hate crimes becomes evident. There are no simple answers to complex issues and questions, but thinking systemically about them is a necessary, and preliminary condition for moving forward toward our new century with humaneness, sensitivity to individuals need for dignity, worth and self-esteem and compassion.

References

Adams, Chris and Moss, Michael (1998, December 24). "The Business Potential of Nursing Homes is Elusive, Vencor Finds". *The Wall Street Journal*: A 1, A 10.

Alexander, F. King (1998, Fall). "Vouchers in American Education: Hard Legal and Policy Lessons From Higher Education". *Journal of Educational Finance*: 177-178.

Anderson, Digby (1998, October 29). " Work Without Virtue, or the Decline of Professionalism". *The Wall Street Journal*: A 22.

Apple, Michael (1996). *Popular Culture, Politics, and the Curriculum"*. New York: Teachers College Press: 88.

Auerbach, Jon G. and Pereira, Joseph (1998, October 9). "With PC Ads on Hold Ziff-Davis Takes a Hit". *Wall Street Journal:* B 1.

Armour, Stephanie (1998, November 6-8). "Workforce Absenteeism Soars 25%, Costs Millions". *USA Today:* 1 A.

Armstrong, C. Michael (1999, March 9). *Straight Talk.* New York, New York: ATT: 4.

Associated Press (1998, January 2). "DuPont to Give Law Schools $10 Million". *The Palm Beach Post*: 15 A.

Baker, Michael (1998, November 17). "The Perfect Wife, Korean-Style". *The Christian Science Monitor*: 1, 10.

Baldauf, Scott (1998, June 12). "School-Voucher Movement Gets Boost From Wisconsin Court". *The Christian Science Monitor:* 14.

Barlett, Donald L. and Steele, James B. (1998, November 9). "Corporate Welfare". *Time:* 36-39.

Bayles, Fred (1999). "Boston Schools Drop Affirmative Action Case, Fearing Wide Impact". *USA Today:* 4 A.

Belsie, Laurent (1998 September 21). "Firms Would Fire Clinton". *Christian Science Monitor:* 11.

Belsie, Laurent (1998, October 13). "New Clout of the Comfortable". *The Christian Science Monitor:* 1, 18.

Belsie, Laurent (1998, August 10). "The Unwritten Code No Longer". *The Christian Science Monitor*: B1, B4.

Brandon, John J. (1998, November 2). "Hedge Fund Bailout a U.S. Double Standard". *The Christian Science Monitor:* 19.

Bumpers, Dale, Senator (1998, Fall). "Address to Faculty and Students". In Old Main, University of Arkansas, Fayetteville.

Bundy, McGeorge (1974, August 24). "After the Deluge, The Covenant". *Saturday Review World*: 114.

Burns, Greg (1998, December 31). "Companies Suffer From Y2K Jitters". *Sun-Sentinel*: 1 D, 8 D.

Carelli, Richard (1998, November 10). "Supreme Court Passes on Vouchers". *Tulsa World:* A 8.

Center for Education Reform (1998, September 9). "Charter School Highlights and Statistics". http://edreform.com/pubs/chglance.htm

Cerf, Christopher and Navasky, Victor (1998). *The Experts Speak: The Definitive Compendium of Authoritative Misinformation.* New York: Villard Books: 81, 230-231, 272, 303.

Chaddock, Gail Russell (1998, November 3). "The Business of Change". *The Christian Science Monitor:* B1, B4, B5.

Challenger, John A. (1998, October). "There Is No Future for the Workplace". *The Futurist: 16-20.*

Chmielewski, Dawn C. (1998, November 29). "Techno-Toddlers: Parents Start Infants Early on PCs, Hoping To Prepare Them for School—and The Real World". *Sun-Sentinel*: 3. F.

Clayton, Mark (1998, August 11). "New College Chiefs Get Survival Tips at Summer Boot Camp". *The Christian Science Monitor*: B 6.

Clinton, William Jefferson (1998, November 23). "Thanksgiving Day, 1998: A Proclamation". *The Christian Science Monitor:* 9.

Collie, Tim (1998, December 16). "Kid Power Moves Modern Market". *Sun-Sentinel*: 26 A.

Coolidge, Shelley Donald (1998, December 7). "They're Baaack: Yikes! It's That Time of Year Again When We Work Our Way Through The Annual Performance Review". *The Christian Science Monitor*: 15, 18.

Combs, Casey (1998, December 6). "Gadgets by Geeks: Computer Engineers Designing Future Cyber Fashions". *Tulsa World*: A 33.

Cousins, Norman (1974 August 24). "Prophecy and Pessimism". *Saturday Review:* 6-7.

Cox, James (1999, January 25). "Fruit War May Hike Price of European Luxuries". *USA Today:* B 1.

Cremin, Lawrence A. (1989). *Popular Education and Its Discontents.* New York: Harper and Row: vi-ix, 78.

Cremin, Lawrence A. (1988). *The American Education: The Metropolitan Experience.* New York: Harper and Row.

Cross, Christopher T. (1999, January 16). "Let Retirees Into The Classroom". *Tulsa World:* G 3.

Cunniff, John (1998, December 6). "Worker Morale On a Downfall". *Northwest Arkansas Times:* D 8.

Clymer, Adam (1998, December 27). "Legacy of 105th To Haunt Congress". *Sun-Sentinel:* 5 A.

Dallas, Sandra (1999, February 1). "A Cyber-Community Grows in Brooklyn". *Business Week:* 4.

DelCour, Julie (1998, September 20). "The Melting Pot: How Will the U.S. Handle True Multiracialism". *Tulsa World:* G 6.

Desruisseaux, Paul (1998, December 11). "2-Year Colleges at the Crest of Wave in U.S. Enrollment by Foreign Students". *The Chronicle of Higher Education:* A 66-A 69.

Deutsch, David (1997). *The Fabric of Reality: The Science of Parallel Universes and Its Implications.* New York: Allen Lane, The Penguin Press: 365-366.

Drinkard, Jim (1998, November 5). "Biggest Spenders Reaped Rewards". *USA Today:* 12 A.

Edwards, Tamala M. (1998, December 21). "What Johnny Can't Read". *Time:* 46, 57.

Edelman, Marian Wright (1998, December). "Protect Our Children". *CDF Reports http:www.childrensdefence.org/voice.html.*

Elder Jr., Robert (1998, November 4). "Plan for 30 Charter Schools Seen as Key Test for State". *Wall Street Journal:* T 1, T 3.

Epstein, Jeffrey H. (1998, October). "Demography: Declining Growth in Population Raises Hopes". *The Futurist:* 8.

Erwin, Chuck (1998, December 13). "Are the Sex Lives of Politicians About to be Fair Game for Press?" *Tulsa World:* A 33.

Feeney, Susan (1998, November 22). "Hassle-Free Help To Be Put To The Test". *The Dallas Morning News:* 1 A, 30 A.

Feldman, Linda (1998, December 23). "Wielding A New Moral Yardstick". *The Christian Science Monitor:* 1, 5.

Fine, Andrea (1998, November 24). "When Web Words Threaten". *The Christian Science Monitor: 3.*

Fisher, George M.C. (1999). *Focus.* Rochester, New York: Kodak 1998 Annual Report: 6.

Flavin, Christopher and Dunn, Seth (1998, December 28). "Action Signals Beginning of Geriatric Ear for Oil Industry". *Sun-Sentinel*: 17Ab.

Forman, Ellen (1998, November 26). "Babies in Workland". *Sun-Sentinel*: 1 D, 8 D.

Forman, Ellen (1998, November 29. "Domestic Partners Make Gains: Companies Extend Benefits As Tool To Recruit and Retain Workers". *Sun-Sentinel*: 1 F, 8 F.

Francis, David R. (1998 November 23). "Capitalism: Tamed But Triumphant". *The Christian Science Monitor*: 10-11.

Fraser, Andrew (1998, October 11). "Hedge Fund Debacle and Questionable Judgment". *Northwest Arkansas Times:* B 9.

Garten, Jeffrey E. (1998, November 9). "Cutting Fat Won't Be Enough to Survive This Crisis". *Business Week*: 26.

Gerstner, Louis V, Jr. (1999). *StartUp.* Armonk, New York: *IBM 1998 Annual Report.* 7-8.

Gillman, Omer (1998 October 12). "Better Things to Do Than Cast Ballot". *Tulsa World:* A 1, A 3.

Gallagher, Leigh (1998, September 7). "Death to the Cubicle". *Forbes*: 54.

Glazer, Nathan (1977). "Introduction: The Business of the Future". In Cullen Murphy editor, *The Third Century: Twenty-Six Prominent Americans Speculate On the Educational Future.* New Rochelle, New York: Change Magazine Press: 1-13.

Gold, Scott (1999, January 2). "Grants Broaden Student's Options: State Helps With Private Education". *Sun-Sentinel*: 1 B, 10 B.

Goodrich, Lawrence, J. (1998, November 24). "American Politics: A Quiet Revolution". *The Christian Science Monitor*: 12-14.

Greene, Maxine (1996, April 10). "Resisting the One-Dimensional Education and Multiplicity". Address to Society of Professors of Education. *American Educational Research Association.* New York City, New York, Sheraton Hotel.

Grier, Peter (1998, October 19). "Why There's So Much Left in Congress's In Box". *The Christian Science Monitor: 3.*

Gross, Ronald and Beatrice (1975, March). "A Nation of Learners". *American Education:* 27.

Gullo, Karen (1999, January 19). "Government Spent $866 Million On Worker Complaints In the Last Decade". *Northwest Arkansas Times:* A 5.

Guy, Kingsley (1998, December 29). "Warranty Idea Might Make High School Diplomas Meaningful". *Orlando Sentinel:* 12 A.

Harrington, Patrick (1998, September 28). "A California Measure Ties Some Teacher's Tongues". *Wall Street Journal:* B 1.

Harwood, John and Cummings, Jeanne (1998, December 11). "Tactical Retreat: One Likely Casuality of the Clinton Years: The Scandal Gambit". *The Wall Street Journal:* A 1, A 6.

Heilbroner, Robert (1961). *The Future As History.* New York: Grove Press: 206, 208-209.

Heilbroner, Robert (1995). *Visions of the Future: The Distant Past, Yesterday, Today, Tomorrow.* New York: Oxford University Press: 95.

Healy, Patrick (1998 February 27). "A 2-Year College in Arizona Bills Itself as a New Model for Public Higher Education". *Chronicle of Higher Education:* A 32.

Hemlock, Doreen (1998, November 28). "Florida Is Paying The Price, Reports Global Woes Hurt Trade" *Sun-Sentinel:* 12 C.

Hendrie, Caroline (1998, December 2). "Sex With Student: When Employees Cross The Line". *Education Week:* 1, 12-17.

Hendrie, Caroline (1998, December 2). "Abuse by Women Raises Its Own Set of Problems", *Education Week:* 1, 14-17.

Hendrie, Caroline (1998, April 29). "Plan for Little Rock Would Shift Away from Busing". *Education Week:* 3.

Henry, Tamara (1999, January 18). "Schools Get a Guide on Behaviors That Cross The Line". *USA Today:* D 1.

Herman, Roger E. and Gioia, Joyce L. (1998, December). "Future-Focused Companies Are Learning That Corporate Responsibilities Extend Beyond Their Own Front Door". *The Futurist:* 26, 35-38.

Higgins, Alexander G. (1999, February 1). "Egyptian President Calls for Rethinking of Free-Market Approach". *Northwest Arkansas Times:* A 10.

"High Court Turns Away Voucher Dispute: Debate Rages On". *Northwest Arkansas Times:* A 8.

Holmstrom, David (1998, October 14). "Court Volunteers Help Rescue Children in Abusive Situations". *The Christian Science Monitor:* B 4.

Holt, Pat M. (1998, September 3). "Population Shifts—Future Challenge is Here". *The Christian Science Monitor:* 11.

Holtz, Lou (1998). *Winning Every Day.* New York: Harper Business/ Harper Collins: 201-202.

Hunter, Kenneth W. (1998, Summer). "Co-Editor's Observations on Communities in Transformation: Strengthening the Foundations of Social Progress". *Futures Research Quarterly:* Vol. 14, No. 1: 21.

Hymowitz, Carol (1998, December 22). "CEOs Set the Tone for How To Handle Questions of Ethics". *The Wall Street Journal:* B 1.

Irwin, Neil (1998, August 24). "Less Loyalty in New American Workplace". *The Christian Science Monitor:* 11.

Isaacson, Walter (1999, January 11). "The Biotech Century". *Time:* 42-43.

Jackson, Derrick Z. (1999, January 24). "Creating, Not Curbing, Poverty". *Tulsa World:* G 1.

Jurgensen, Karen (1998, December 24). "HMOs Lured Elderly Into Fold, Now Abandon Them to Uncertainty". *USA Today:* 9 A.

Kahn, Charles N. III (1998, December 24). "Government Rules Burdensome". *USA Today:* 9 A.

Karmatz, Laura and Labi, Aisha (1998, November 9). "States At War". *Time:* 40, 54.

Kilpatrick, James J. (1998, February 16). "Sex and the Court". *Tulsa World:* A 10.

Kirchner, Jake (1999, April 6). "Amazon Muddies Its Waters". *PC Magazine:* 30.

Kissel, Kelly P. (1998, October 12). "Bumpers' Final Speech to Senate Laments Six Years of Investigation". *Northwest Arkansas Times:* A 1, A 6.

Kronholz, June (1999, January 12). "Learning Curve: Charter Schools Begin To Prod Public Schools Toward Competition". *The Wall Street Journal:* A 1.

Kronholz, June (1998, May 28). "Chary Schools Tell Teachers, 'Don't Touch, Don't Hug'". *Wall Street Journal:* B 1.

Kronholz, June (1998, November 10). "Wisconsin School Voucher Plan is Upheld". *The Wall Street Journal:* A 2.

Kronholz, June (1998, December 23). "States Take Lead in National Tests for Schoolchildren". *The Wall Street Journal*: A 16.

Lampman, Jane (1998 May 28). "Fostering Trust and Civility Is a Moral Issue". *The Christian Science Monitor:* B 3.

Lampman, Jane (1998, December 10). "Gallup Surveys the Surge in Spirituality". *The Christian Science Monitor*: 12.

Landay, Jonathan (1997, September 12). "Values Training: Cure for Army Harassment?" *The Christian Science Monitor*: 3.

Lardner, James (1998, December 14). "Cupid's Cubicles: Office Romance Is Alive and Well, Despite a Barrage of Corporate Countermeasures". *U.S. News and World Report*: 44, 46-49, 51-54.

Leavitt, Paul (1998, November 20). "Capital Roundup: Civility Retreat". *USA Today*: 8 A.

Lee, Jessica and Puente, Maria (1998, November 5). "Women, Minorities Propelled Democrats in Key Races". *USA Today:* 2 A.

Levy, Steven (1998, December 7). "Xmas.com". *Newsweek:* 50, 56.

Lohr, Steve and Markoff, John (1998, December 28). "Computing's Next Wave Is Nearly At Hand". *New York Times*: C 1, C 3.

Lublin, Joann S. (1998, December 24). "Expatriates Go That Extra Mile". *The Wall Street Journal* : B 1.

Lynn, Barry W. (1998, June 29). "Church-State Breach Perils Public Schools". *Sun-Sentinel:* 7A.

Maharaz, Davan (1998, November 29). "Firms Downsize in Good Times, Too". *Sun-Sentinel*: 1 F, 2 F.

Maynard, Rebecca A. (1997). *Kids Having Kids: Economic Costs and Social Consequences of Teen Pregnancy.* Washington, D.S. The Urban Institute Press: 1.

Marquez, Myriam (1998). "Soft Money: The Real Scandal". *Tulsa World:* G 6.

Marriott, J.W. Jr. (1999, March 5). *Marriott International 1998 Annual Report.* Washington, D.C. Marriott International: 5, 12.

Maxon, Terry (1998, November 22). "American Aims To Be Kinder, Gentler". *The Dallas Morning News:* 1 H, 7 H.

Mauro, Tony (1998, November 10). "Court Allows School Vouchers". *USA Today:* 1A, 4 A.

McLaughlin, Abraham (1998, August 28). "Long Workdays Draw Backlash". *The Christian Science Monitor:* 1,11.

"Medicare Report Due" (1998, December 26). *Sun-Sentinel*: 10 C.

Mellor, William (1998, June 29). "School Choice Benefits Poor, Minorities". *Sun Sentinel:* 7 A.

Meyers, Bill (1998 October 9). "Global Crisis Triggers Job Cuts, Buyouts". *USA Today:* Section B: 1.

Meyer, Michael (1998, December 14). "Oh No, Here We Go Again: Health Care Costs Are Soaring and Companies Are Passing the Increases Along to Their Workers". *Newsweek*: 46, 47.

Molitor, Graham T.T. (1998, August-September). "Trends and Forecasts for the New Millennium". *The Futurist*: 53-59.

Moseley, Ray (1999, May 26). "Language Struggle Leaves Lives Lost in Translation". *Sun-Sentinel*: 14 A.

Munk, Nina (1999, February 1). "Finished At Forty". *Fortune*: 50-53.

Mulholland, Loria A. and Bierlein, Louann A. (1997). "Charter Schools" in editor Walling Donovan R. *Hot Buttons:* 85-114. (1997).

Newcomb, Amelia (1998, October 13). "Weighing In on Diversity". *The Christian Science Monitor:* 7.

Novak, Kindsey (1998 September 20). "Loose Talk". *Chicago Tribune:* Section 6: 5.

Nye, Erle (1999). *The New TXU: Our Sound Strategy.* Fort Worth, Texas: Texas Utilities Corporation: 4, 5.

O'Dell, Larry (1998, December 22). "Schools May Pay if Grads Not Ready". *Sun- Sentinel*: 9 A.

Owens, Tom (1998). "Educational Reform in Latin America". Paper presented at the *American Educational Studies Association Meeting*, Philadelphia, Pennsylvania, November 4-7, 1998.

Page, Susan (1998, October 13). "Leaders Peer Ahead to New Millennium". *USA Today:* 6A – 8A.

Peterson, Scott (1999, February 17). "Barbie Struts Into an Islamic Stronghold". *The Christian Science Monitor*: 1, 7.

Pierce, Wendell (1975). "America's Evolving Role". *American Education:* 28.

Platt, Kevin (1998, December 31). "China Hits at E-Mail to Curb Dissent". *The Christian Science Monitor*: 1, 7.

Quintanilla, Carol (1998, October 16). "Broad Round of Job Cuts Expected in The U.S.". *Wall Street Journal:* A 2, A 6.

Reardon, Patrick T. and Obejas, Achy (1999, March 21). "Putting a Face On The Numbers". *Chicago Tribune*: Section 13, 5.

Recer, Paul (1999, January 22). "Researchers Able to Change Cells' Function, Raising Hope of New Way to Grow Organs". *Northwest Arkansas Times*: A 12.

Ridenour, Army (1998, December 28). "Should Exxon and Mobil Be Allowed To Merge? Consumers Won't Be Hurt; Doomsayers Never Seem To Catch Up With Predictions". *Sun-Sentinel*: 17 A.

Rofes, Eric (1998, April). *How Are School Districts Responding to Charter Laws and Charter Schools?* Berkeley, California: University of California: 1-2.

Romanos, Sue (1998, December 28). "Alternative Workers Let Firm Boost Staff". *Sun-Sentinel*: 7.

Rutledge, John (1998 September 7). "One Man's Poison". *Forbes*: 250.

Rubin, Rita (1998, December 8). "One Couple's Surplus Can Fill Void of Another". *USA Today*: 1 A, 2 A.

Rule, James B. (1998, October 6). "Privacy in an Information Age". *The Christian Science Monitor:* 11.

Salzman, Marian and Matathia, Ira (1998, June-July). "Lifestyles of the Next Millennium: 65 Forecasts". *The Futurist:* Insert 1-5.

Sandberg, Jared (December 7, 1998). "Net Gain". *Newsweek:* 46, 48-49.

Sandler, Linda (1998, October 14). "Reading, Writing and Building: Nation's Elite Schools Market Tony Improvements to Lure Students". *The Wall Street Journal:* B 12.

Schaefer, Naomi (1998, November 4). "The Bard, Barred". *The Wall Street Journal*: A22.

Scherer, Ron (1998, December 4). "Rise of the Mega-Firm: Is Bigger Really Better?". *The Christian Science Monitor*: 1, 5.

Schmitt, Richard (1998, October 9). "In U.S. Courts, The Whole Truth is Often Nothing But". *Wall Street Week*: B: 1.

Schultz, Ellen E. (1998, December 18). "Some Workers Facing Pension Hit". *The Wall Street Journal*: C 1.

Sennett, Richard (1998). *The Corrosion of Capitalism: The Personal Consequences of Work in the New Capitalism.* New York: W.W. Norton.

Shlaes, Amity (1998 October 1). "School Choice Isn't A New Idea". *The Wall Street Journal:* A 22.

Simpson, Jeff (1998, November 12). "Flawed Concept: Forcing Public Schools to 'Compete'". *The Christian Science Monitor*: 11.

Sirico, Robert A (1998, November 18). "Human Failure Isn't Market Failure". *Wall Street Journal:* A 22.

Sklar, Holly (1998, November 22). "Whose Welfare? Hunger On Rise While Corporate Breaks Keep Rolling Along". *Sun-Sentinel*: 19 A.

Slambrouck, Paul Van (1998, November 27). "Gazing Into the Next Millennium". *The Christian Science Monitor*: 1, 4.

Solomon, Robert C. (1998, February 27). "Is It Ever Right to Lie? The Philosophy of Deception". *The Chronicle of Higher Education:* A 60.

"Some Facts About the Flow of People Into the U.S.". (1998, October 4). *Northwest Arkansas Times:* C 1. (U.S. Department of Justice, 1996 Statistical Yearbook of the Immigration and Naturalization Service and Population Reports from the U.S. Department of Commerce, 1996 and 1997).

Spotts, Peter N. (1998, November 6). "Embryo-Based Research: Advances and Argument". *The Christian Science Monitor:* 3.

Stead, Deborah (1998, November 8). "Bent Out of Shape by Flexibility". *The New York Times*: 6.

Stepanek, Marcia (November 9, 1998). "2000 Reasons to Celebrate: For Lawyers, The Millennium Bug is a Godsend". *Business Week:* 54.

Stevenson, Richard W. (1999, January 6). "Texaco Is Said to Set Payment Over Sex Bias". *Tulsa World*: C 1.

Stewart, Donald M. (1998, October). "Freshmen Set Records in Diversity, Grades". *National Association of Student Personnel Administrators*: 1,7.

Stone, George C. (1997). "Interdependence in Dewey's Theory of Community". In Van Patten, James, Stone, George C. and Ge Chen. *Individual and Collective Contributions Toward Humaneness in Our Time:* 23-24.

Talbott, Stephen L. (1995). *The Future Does Not Compute.* Sebastopol, California: O' Reilly and Associates: 360, 383.

Tannen, Deborah (1998). *The Argument Culture: Moving From Debate to Dialogue.* New York: Random House: 131.

Tannenbaum, Jeffrey A. (1999, January 12). "Small Companies Find New Way to Retain Employees". *The Wall Street Journal*: B 2.

Taranto, James (1998, December 22). "The Real Sexual McCarthyites Back Clinton". *The Wall Street Journal*: A 18.

Thau, Richard D. and Heflin, Jay S. editors. (1997). *Generations Apart: Xers vs. Boomers vs. The Elderly.* New York: Prometheus Books. Cited in "Demography: X'ers vs. Boomers". *Futurist:* 8-9.

"The State of America's Children Yearbook (1998). *Children Defense Fund:* http://www.childrensdefense.org/moreinfo.html.

Turbak, Gary (1999, January). "Tomorrow's Brainchild: The First Years Last Forever". *Kiwanis*: 26-29, 50.

Tyson, James L. (1998, November 23). "Internet Sales to Reach New Highs". *The Christian Science Monitor*: 15.

Tyson, Ann Scott (1998, October 8). "Why Congress Budget Train Is Seldom On Time". *The Christian Science Monitor:* 3.

Valdmanis, Thor (1998, December 1). "Oil Merger Could Cost 12,000 Jobs". *USA Today:*1 A.

Van Patten, James and Fisher, Bill (1997). "Veblen's Views on Society and Education". In *Watersheds in Higher Education*: 173-182.

Van Patten, James, Stone, George and Ge Chen (1997). *Individual and Collective Contributions to Humaneness in Our Time.* Lanham, Maryland: University Press of America: 1-8.

Waldheim, Kurt (1974, August 24). "Toward Global Interdependence". *Saturday Review World*: 63.

Walker, Ruth (1999, January 9, April 5). "Canadian Inuit Help Out Their Russian Kin". And "For Canada's Inuits, This Land is Our Land (Nunavut)". *The Christian Science Monitor*: 8, 10.

Walters, Laurel Shaper (1997, March 3). "Proliferation of Charter Schools Signals Their Growing Success". *The Christian Science Monitor:* 12.

Wayne, Leslie (1998 November 8). "The Price of a Vote". *The New York Times:* 4.

Wildstrom, Stephen H. (1998, November 9). "The Last Days of the Home PC?". *Business Week*: 34.

Wingert, Pat, Springen, Karen, Angell, Elizabeth and Meyer, Michael (1998, November 2). "Tomorrow's Child". *Newsweek*: 54,56-58, 61-64.

Weisbrot, Mark (1999, January 3). "Rethink Rush to Globalization". *Sun-Sentinel*: 7 G.

Wood, Daniel B. (1998, June 2). "Arizona's Big Stakes in Charter Schools". *The Christian Science Monitor:* 1, 10.

Wynter, Leon E. (1999, January 6). "Companies Try a New Tool To Bring Diversity Home". *The Wall Street Journal*: B1.

Yaukey, John (1999, January 12). "Taking Technology From Here to the Infinitesimal". *USA Today*: 6 D.

Some Reflections on Media and the Future

Frontiers of Media Futures

Technological discoveries break new frontiers every day. Cyborgs or beings that are transformed humans, created by odd marriages of flesh and technology, mutants constructed by accident or design into a new shape, are now coming to life in the university, according to Edward Rothstein (1995). He notes that they embody all the anxieties, dreams and textual technologies that mark so much contemporary academic work. Rothstein found a number of papers, articles and books being written about Cyborgs and that Nicholas Negroponte, founding director of M.I.T's Media Lab, in his best selling book *Being Digital* argues that digital technology will break down all distinctions between text, sound and image, between television, computer and audio systems. Negroponte believes these worlds will mutate and a stream of bits will enter our lives to be interpreted by intelligent boxes that can store and translate the data, turning them into information and entertainment.

At mid-2000, the rapidity of change in the field of technology has blurred distinctions between the computer, telephones, cell phones, wireless, broadband systems, the Internet, television, and film, as interconnections, interdependence, and global innovation merge. Although there are many varying viewpoints about the U.S. Justice Department and 19 states attorney general's suing Microsoft Corporation for violating federal antitrust laws, a growing number of analysts question America's judicial systems ability to keep up with the Computer Age. As Van Slambrouck (2000) points out, in the two years since the Microsoft case went to trial, the technology landscape has changed so significantly that some see the ruling as having less and less practical impact, making it difficult to find effective remedies. Van Slambrouck continued by noting that the skyrocketing importance of the Internet and proliferation of computer rivals, such as smart phones and Palm Pilots has already surpassed Microsoft's dominance.

Meanwhile mergeomanic among media corporations continue at a dizzying pace. Lawrence (2000) writes of the trend toward consolidation, convergence and crossover. Viacom buys CBS, Dow Jones, NBC, MSNBC, CNBC, Microsoft, all work together while Disney owns the Mighty Ducks, ABC, ESPN, the Kentucky Prairie Farmer and Women's Wear Daily. Lawrence believes we are witnessing the greatest media explosion in history not just on the web but in digital TV channels, satellite radio, even magazine titles. Bell South and SBC are joining forces to expand cell phone access. ATT, Sprint, MCI have been on a buying spree, merging, consolidating and expanding their reach into technology, entertainment and marketing.

Electronic Books

Writing about technology in an arena where six months makes for obsolescence, is a challenge. One can predict with some degree of certainty that in the future information access systems will be much easier, simpler to use than is indicated in this book. Akst (1998) found an Internet technological revolution will provide electronic books which together with low cost printing will change the way we read. Books can be bought by downloading. The books are encoded so they will only work on an individual's machine. The back-lit screen was fairly easy to see when switched to the large-type option. Akst continued by noting the text can be underlined and searched, and that battery life was impressive. Recharging, like downloading books was easy using the cradle and cable for a personal computer. Naisbitt (1994) in his *Global Paradox* stated that as technology empowers individuals, it creates greater opportunities for us all. He further finds that the marketplace will become even more efficient because of the availability of timely, uncensored information. That, he finds, will almost certainly put the bureaucracies, both in government and commerce, out of business.

Campbell (2000) discussed a new Stephen King short story that was published only on the Net. King's e-ghost story "Riding the Bullet" was so popular among his fans, that computer access was delayed at times. Microsoft officials, Campbell reported, predicts that by 2020, 90 percent of all titles will be sold in electronic rather than paper form.

Monitoring the information sources for accuracy, and quality is vital. Thousands of students, business, and industrial managers and workers at home and abroad often place too much faith in the reliability, and accuracy of Internet information to their detriment. The information age is evolving so rapidly it has been difficult to monitor quality. Government and corporate efforts are currently underway to trace and incarcerate hackers who have threatened information access through attempts to destroy Internet providers networks and crash computer hard drives.

Americans are increasingly gadget happy. New computers, cellular phones, sound systems, televisions with VCR's, C.D. ROM's are just a few of the gadgets becoming part of everyone's repertoire. Years ago, Charlie Chaplin was in a film entitled *New Times* which was a parody about American fascination with technology. Holden (1996, January 8) discusses the work of Katsuhiro Otomo, one of Japan's leading creators of animated films who has developed a futuristic morality tale *RoujinZ* in which he introduces a gadget designed to answer every need one could think of or imagine. The movie provides insights into the human condition in an ever-more gadget oriented society. And an increasing number of individuals establish relationships through the Internet.

The film *You've Got Mail* identifies the power of the chat room Internet in cyberspace (Morgenstern, 1998). So all pervasive have Internet chat rooms become on college campuses that some universities have counseling for those students so obsessed with the Internet that they miss classes and often have serious health problems. Underlying messages of Chaplin's, and Katsuhiro's work is Americans' passion for speed, efficiency and machines. The message also includes the deep-seated search for cheap, quick technological fixes or short term answers to complex problems. The media reflects the society it interprets and thus represents the one-minute sound bites, the repeated messages designed to get voters to support candidates for reelection or to sell all manner of merchandise. The quality, accuracy, and truthfulness of information disseminated is often a casualty of the focus on speed, efficiency and getting the sound bite that will move individuals to action.

Privacy and Media Images

A recent Hollywood film *The Enemy of the State* depicted the dangers of a gadget-oriented society where individual privacy is threatened by a multitude of clever listening devices. The real life experience of Monica Lewinsky whose secretly taped conversations with Linda Tripp were broadcast throughout the world, demonstrated the danger to individual freedoms of misuse of technology. An unelected overzealous prosecutor may be able to gather information detrimental to a president or any elected official. When Kenneth Starr, the prosecutor in the Clinton saga, felt the media was denigrating his work, and image, he hired a public relations firm to help him develop a more humane media image. Thurman (1998) reported on the success of the strategic effort to rehabilitate Starr's public image including training to appear more causual, warm and open through informal dress and behavior. These efforts illustrate the power of the media in American society. Lurid sexual details, adding up to world class smut, were displayed in excruciating detail for the whole world to see (Neal, 1998). The resulting impeachment hearings during the 1998 Christmas and New Year Season, were a circus of Congressperson's seeking to convince the public through media communications networks of the absolute, unequivocal rightness and morality of their position. Final voting represented clear partisanship in both theory and practice. Meanwhile talking heads dominated television broadcasts under the daily heading of *White House in Crisis.* The Clinton-Lewinsky liaison led to a heyday for reporters, commentators, and legislators, all trying to get in the act through spinning or embellishing the story lines. Gridlock occurred as partisan politics took center stage in an ever-unfolding drama while the nation's business ground to a halt. Reporters often yelled "are you planning to resign or what is your continued relationship with Monica Lewinsky", whenever the President was giving a press conference or attending a meeting.

Media Scandals

Harwood and Cummins (1998) pointed to the crescendo of a generation of scandal-driven American politics, built on partisan hatreds, an avid press corps and a hair trigger independent counsel law, which turned allegation of ethical lapses into everyday weapons. Harwood and Cummins referred to author Suzanne Garment's perception that there was a self-reinforcing scandal machine composed of journalists, ambitious prosecutors, vengeful congressional staffers and ideologically driven lobbying groups. Both media elites and political opponents hired investigators to dig up as much dirt on a candidate as possible. As we near the 21st century, a legacy for the future may well be continuing incivility, personal destruction, mudslinging, and governmental gridlock.

John Towers, Clarence Thomas, Newt Gingrich, Gary Hart, Henry Hyde, Dan Burton, Helen Chenoweth and Bob Livingston, most elected Congresspersons and Senators, as well as a Supreme Court appointee, are examples of scandal tactics either destroying careers or spotlighting past behaviors that threaten personal careers, reputations, honor, integrity and individual dignity. With media feeding the appetite for scandal there is a trend to scorched earth, smear, fear, fratricide and hypocrisy policies.

Hustler magazine publisher Larry Flynt, in an effort to highlight Republican Congresspersons hypocrisy condemning sexual behavior of the President, offered $1 million for information on sexual skeletons from their past that could be verified. Long term Congressman Bob Livingston's resignation was the first to be exposed by Flynt's initiative with more certain to follow (Page, 1998). A troubling aspect of Flynt's action was the possibility of manipulation and unintended consequences of fringe, marginalized magazine editors like *Hustler* influencing mainstream journalism with its 24 hour news cycles. Wall-to-wall media coverage of alleged political miscreancy gives birth to a 24-hour Scandal Channel on Cable TV, Web sites, tabloid and mainstream press (Feldmann, 1998). Sensationalism, sex, continues to sell newspapers and often monopolize topics of television talk shows.

Journalistic Credibility

Harwood and Cummins reported that journalistic credibility suffered a series of blows during the coverage of the Lewinisky story with a recent Gallup Poll indicating a third of Americans now believe media scrutiny gets in the way of politicians doing their jobs rather than deterring wrong doing. The proliferation of media outlets, a hunger for selling stories to gain a greater market share place a premium on sensational coverage that political scandals can provide.

Harwood and Cummins found that from Internet gossips to prime time network shows, an environment and culture exists that depends on scandal for its existence. The electorate eventually may tire of sensationalism, turn off and tune out of the age of journalistic excesses and require increased vigor in media monitoring. Meanwhile educators of the future will teach students critical viewing skills and the importance of analysis of media reports in all their various avenues and networks.

Holmstrom (1998) interviewed Pete Hamill, long time *New York Post* writer, and author of *News Is a Verb: Journalism at the End of the Twentieth Century.* Hamill stressed that newspaper journalists need to be calm during the excitement of new breaking gossip and make additional calls to verify facts from rumors to get as close to the truth as possible. Editors have to trust reporters and visa versa.

Balz (1998) noted that the politics of polarization, slinging unfounded accusations, misinformation, disinformation over multimedia systems tends to win elections. He continued by noting that the elements of this style of politics are common to an increasingly disconnected country: negative campaigns, relentless exposure of private lives of politicians, a political system corrupted by huge amounts of money, war-room politics, government by permanent campaign, accelerated news cycles and a destroy your opponent mentality.

Ravitch (1998) reported on an American Association of University Women publication based on spinning and false information. The editors of the AAUW publication reported that schools were heedlessly crushing girls self-esteem and seventy percent of the teachers were giving boys more attention. In addition, the editors of the publication reported that schools discouraged girls from taking math and science courses they would need to compete in the future. Ravitch reported that U.S. Department of Education research studies demolished the AAUW's findings. Ravitch found the most shameful aspect of AAUW's phony, made up crisis, and of the media's gullibility in turning it into conventional wisdom diverted attention from the genuine gaps in American education, which are not between boys and girls but rather among racial groups.

An unfortunate offshoot of excesses in media spinning, and of a fragmented society, has been the acceptance of misrepresentations and embellishing stories. Political correctness has led to accepting inaccuracies in reporting by indigenous authors particularly when dealing with issues of past injustices. Estrada (1998) reported on serious inaccuracies and misrepresentations in Rigoberta Menchu's autobiography. She was awarded the Nobel Peace Prize in 1992. Geir Lundestad, director of the Norwegian Nobel Institute stated that Menchu's prize was not based exclusively or primarily on the autobiography and all autobiographies embellish to a greater or lesser extent. Estrada disagrees with Lundestad and continued by noting that Menchu's deception in her *I, Rigoberta Menchu* was a disservice to the future needs of indigenous peasants. People may question the aggrievement of indigenous peoples and their legitimate needs to relate true details of their personal and collective sufferings.

As we find the explosion of technological advances impinging on every channel of communication in our lives, it is important to analyze the quality of the information disseminated and received. Government officials frequently use polling experts to determine what issues to address in order to prepare for reelection. Single interest groups often are overzealous in pushing their causes to the detriment of the common good. Frequently exaggeration is employed to create fear in and win points with the voting public. As the nation faces increased challenges to fulfill political promises, prioritizing expenditures creates landmines. Toy (1996, January 8) notes that New York City public officials find it difficult to raise taxes for education when promises were made to increase the size of the police force under a Safe Streets, Safe City program policy. Determining whether new taxes for education should go into repairing decaying schools or for teacher salaries often leads to the branding of scapegoats. Generally inefficient bureaucracies are blamed for misuse of resources utilizing all available media channels to disseminate the information.

The Many Faces of the Media

Sissela Bok in her *Lying: Moral Choice in Public and Private Life* (1978) exploring Montaigne's Essays noted that "if like truth, the lie had but one face, we would be on better terms. For we would accept as certain the opposite of what the liar would say. But the reverse of truth has a hundred thousand faces and an infinite field." Bok also wrote that the awareness that everything in life and experience connects, that all is a seamless web so that nothing can be said without qualifications and elaborations in infinite regress results in a sense of lassitude stealing over even the most intrepid.

Bok refers to the oft repeated phase in our courts "the truth, the whole truth, and nothing but the truth." She notes that the intentional manipulation of information is a challenge to our social order (p. 8). We live in a time when harm done to the public trust can be noted first-hand. Ethical issues such as Watergate, Whitewatergate, deceit through use of high sounding aims such as "national security" or the "adversary system of justice," are examples where officials provided disinformation for what seemed to them, at the time, good reasons (p.27). An example of disinformation was Lyndon Johnson's reelection team working overtime to portray Senator Barry Goldwater as an irresponsible hawk who would escalate the war in Vietnam.

Kaul (1998) discussed the credibility gap among writers and reporters. Columnists are more frequently being fired for falsifying news in their reports. Examples include the *Boston Globe*'s firing of

Patricia Smith, a Pulitzer Prize finalist and columnist who invented information to embellish her story. *The New Republic's* editors sought Stephen Glass's resignation for making up entire articles and passing them off for hard fact. Kaul found that there is no story so biased or flimsy that it can't find its way into the mainstream press, so long as it first appears on the Internet, where standards of taste, accuracy and verifiability are nonexistent. Matt Drudge, who runs a popular Internet "news" site, is often a quoted in newspaper and magazine columns without any verification of his material. Kaul pointed to the Monica Lewinsky spectacle to demonstrate how news gathering organizations are rushing to print and broadcast rumors, innuendom and unsubstantiated gossip. This is an emerging phenomena, due in part, to the rush to print material that will increase circulation. Perhaps editors should improve their own performance rather than firing overworked columnists desperate for an idea. Meanwhile the credibility of the press in the United States is at an all time low, according to Kaul, a columnist for the Des Moines Register.

The congressional elections of 1998 were inundated with sexual McCarthyism. Weinberg (1998) discussed how most journalists covering the Bill Clinton-Monica Lewinsky sexual relationship showed their lack of concern for authentication by printing rumors from unnamed sleazy sources, rather than in good ethical, reporting. Weinberg highlights major points in Richard Reeves' (1998) book *What the People Know: Freedom and the Press*. Reeves found that Internet journalist Matt Drudge placed many Clinton-Lewinsky rumors on his web site. Reeves noted that hacks and hackers, dumped information as raw as sewage on the American public which, in turn, was often quoted by national news reporters. It demonstrated the power of scandal to sell papers, to increase television viewing and to heighten the competitiveness of reporters after a hot story.

Richey (1999) reported that ride-alongs (reporters, photographers, television news crews accompanying law enforcement officers as they conduct a search or make an arrest) often provide for television shows like COPS. These television shows serve the publics' appetite for gritty "in-your-face" scenes between police and suspects. Several lawsuits are pending due to invasion of privacy, law enforcement officer's use of excessive force, and entering the wrong house in search of a criminal. The Supreme Court will continue to face issues of invasion of privacy and First Amendment's right to know. Many news reporters often seem to be more interested in entertainment than in public service or protecting a suspect's rights.

Lyndon Johnson professed repeatedly to be a candidate of peace. His ploy worked, and after he was reelected he supported escalation of the war in Vietnam with the massive bombing raids over North Vietnam through "Operation Thunder." Governmental advisors and Johnson believed what they did was best for the country, and operated on the basis of distortion and disinformation. They feared an informed public would not support the war's escalation (p. 171-172).

Franklin D. Roosevelt while campaigning for reelection in 1940 said, "I have said this before, but I shall say it again and again and again: Your boys are not going to be sent into any foreign wars" (p. 179). Both presidents feared the electorate would not support going to war. Then and now, media channels disseminate information designed to gain public support for war efforts.

Ware and Straus (2000) addressed media bias in the international arena. Western journalists find the popularity of the war in Chechnya in Russia is due to official repression and manipulation of the media. Human rights organizations interview displaced Chechen refugees while failing to interview Dagestani refugees or victims of the widespread kidnapping industry. Thus there is a lopsided reporting where no one gets a balanced picture, rhetoric intensifies, security relations deteriorate and biases are reinforced. Ware and Straus found that more than 1,300 Russian civilians, men, women, children, Christian, Muslim, light-skinned, dark skinned, have been held in Chechen cellars under exceptionally brutal circumstances. Ware and Straus noted that no Western media outlets reported that the supreme Islamic leader of Chechnya, Mufti Akhmed Kahdzhi Kadyrov said on February 7, 2000 that Russian occupation is necessary to protect the people from violent civil strife at the hands of Chechnya's warlords. By omission Western reporters too often write simplistic accounts of complex issues in the International arena. Then their biased reports are distributed widely throughout the world.

President Clinton's military advisors recommended bombing of Iraq for failing to live up to the agreement to have United Nations inspectors search for hidden lethal weapons of mass destruction—missiles, chemical plants, and storage points. Although some news analysts disputed the rationale for the Iraq policy, a couple of days prior to his impeachment vote in Congress, Clinton (on the recommendation of his military, state department and White House intelligence staffs,) ordered the bombing of Iraq. It was timed to avoid the holy period of Ramadanm so important in Arab nations. So fragmented, divided, and polarized was the Congress, that the majority party engaged in impeachment deliberations while military action was being conducted. Some Congressmen and some media questioned the President's leadership policy at this critical time. The majority party used multimedia communications networks, to proselytize the public on supporting impeachment proceedings based on lying under oath about a sexual escapade, while, at the same time, applauding their new majority leader for admitting to adulterous affairs during his thirty-three year marriage. The incoming house speaker spoke of his search for spiritual counseling and forgiveness and noted that he had informed reporters that he was "running for speaker, not sainthood" and that "there was a reason for those words" (Clines, 1998). The chair of the Congressional impeachment proceedings which made it clear that reference to sexual indiscretions of any member of the house of representatives would not be appropriate, was received by the boos from the opposition party. As the Christmas, 1998, season neared, President William Jefferson Clinton was impeached by the majority party of Congress. Some individuals refer to an emerging ethic: the politics of destruction utilizing the power of the press, television, the Internet and film. *Wag The Dog*, a Hollywood film portraying the government creating a fictional war in the media, was cited in a multitude of attacks on the president's character, values, and ethics. The new century ushered in a continued attack on the president, who survived the impeachment process, but was impeded in executive work by animosity of his adversaries even to the point of rejecting treaties to control nuclear proliferation supported by other nation's and other efforts to foster world peace. Both political parties used the media in a game of one-up-man-ship.

Weinberg (1998) analyzed Richard Reeves book *What the People Know: Freedom and The Press*, Harvard University Press. Reeves believes many journalists have no idea of how to ferret out the truth, or seem to have forgotten that it is part of their job. Many members of the press have never honed interviewing skills, have little knowledge of shorthand to assist in accurate note taking, know little about locating or analyzing revelatory public records and are not computer literate. Journalists, according to Reeves too often accept their sources' self-interested versions without checking further. This leads to allowing rumors, trial balloons, and personal agendas to reach the public disguised as apparent fact.

Reeves found that "pseudojournalist" Matt Drudge used the Internet to spread information regardless of factual accuracy. Assuming 10% of the information was true, or 95% of it was true, the question of which of it was true, the question of which 10% or which 95%, was generally left to the imagination.

Information Censorship

The press has a moral and ethical obligation to disseminate information to the public. Moffet (1996) notes however that a free press has been a challenge to military and government officials who often engage in censorship on the basis of "national interest and security." Moffet reported Gen. William Tecumseh Sherman bellowed to his staff that it is impossible to carry on a "war with a free press." Today in the Balkans or other areas of conflict, the free press pushes to increase the circulation of their newspapers and television stations, while their intense scrutiny of day to day operations can jeopardize military missions. With hundreds or thousands of journalists competing for stories, every casualty or military setback can take a toll on public and congressional support for operations abroad, according to defense experts. Brookings Institution defense analysts find when the media reports on the horrible things happening in areas like the Balkan, it puts pressure on the President to do something that might lead to a military quagmire like Vietnam.

When the media reports on the horrors of a military operation including collateral damage information, it puts pressure on the president to get out the full facts of the operation regardless of possible harm to American troops. Currently with intense media interest in military operations, top officials provide unparalleled access for reporters. The new system is very much like a Madison Avenue manual for a publicity blitz. The military provides more pictures and quotes than can possibly be used, according to retired Admiral William Lawrence, co-author of a report on the military and the media, *America's Team: The Odd Couple,* but they are military reports (Moffett, 1996) often justifying actions that have led to collateral damage. Pinpoint accuracy in missile bombing is assured prior to such action, but after news reports point to civilian causalities, military officials confirm such mishaps.

Terrorism

Van Atta (1998) reported on the need for responsible media coverage of international terrorism. *The Chicago Sun-Times* and *Daily News* have established standards which include paraphrasing terrorist demands to avoid unbridled propaganda, banning reporters from getting involved in negotiations with terrorists, giving senior supervisory editors in touch with police authorities that final call on the stories and aiming at thoughtful, restrained and credible coverage of terrorist acts. Van Atta noted the difficulty of balancing necessary freedom of the press and national interests in protecting citizens from terrorist games. He referred to Prime Minister Margaret Thatcher, comments about finding ways to starve the terrorist and the hijacker of the oxygen of publicity on which they depend. Van Atta noted that there may come a day, not far off, when the U.S. government and other democratic nations impose censorship or even martial law, because terrorists have obtained or used biological, chemical, or nuclear weapons. Van Atta continued by making the comparison—if publicity is the life-blood of terrorists, news is the lifeblood of liberty. The issue of information control and media responsibility is the challenge of our age as both international and internal threats to citizens and civilization increase.

As Van Atta noted Osama bin Laden would be only a backwater terrorist if Clinton had not identified him publicly and spent over $100 million to bomb his country's infrastructure. Van Atta cautioned media to be most vigilant in making unfounded assumptions or attempting to brand any major group with the acts of a few malcontents. A few examples of this problem included self-avowed Christians bombing abortion clinics, the Aum Shinrikyou cult in Japan mangling Buddhist teachings to justify a series of nerve gas attacks on innocents in Japanese subways, or two Jewish groups that have been labeled terrorist by the Israeli government, which also condemned the Jewish terrorist who attacked a mosque at Hebron and another who assassinated Prime Minister Yitzhak Rabin in the name of God.

Guelke (1998) reminded us that the cruelty of terrorist crimes should not blind us to the reality that, for the majority of Third World citizens, lethal political violence commonly forms a terrifying background to daily life. Guelke gave the example that by the time the first Western hostage was seized in Lebanon in 1982, thousands of ordinary Lebanese had already been abducted and murdered by the contending militias in Lebanon's civil war, but given the focus on Western victims, such everyday brutality remains all but forgotten. Part of the reason for the focus on Western victims is the more sophisticated, technologically modern facilities and funding available to Western media reporters.

Guelke noted the acts of indiscriminate violence are often committed by the uncontrollable fringe elements of terrorist groups. Guelke reported that the Clinton administration was recently criticized by Raymond Seitz, former American ambassador in Britain, for breaking America's established rules of counter-terrorism, in its policy towards Northern Ireland by not negotiating with terrorists and isolating them. While Seitz was correct in stating that the granting of a visa to Gerry Adams in advance of an IRA cease-fire was a breach of rules, he failed to recognize that the risks taken by the Clinton administration enabled a successful peace process. There are no easy answers to the problem of international terrorism, but governments are becoming better prepared to deal with the challenge.

Futurists Alvin and Heidi Toffler (1998) find that the United States has Hollywood and CNN, the most powerful, pervasive media in the world. The Toffler's note that Arabs and others often believe news reports reflect official government policy, not understanding the functioning of a free press in an open society. The Internet provides opportunities for anyone to have access to information. Multimedia communication systems break any centralized attempt to control or manipulate information. The Soviets attempt to control information was unsuccessful, and set back innovation and technical progress essential for success the 21st century.

A recent Associated Press article identified past and present presidential concerns with the press. Roosevelt once awarded a reporter the German Iron Cross for giving aid and comfort to the enemy through his typewriter. Truman once wrote to a music critic who panned his daughter Margaret's professional singing career: "I never met you, but if I do you'll need a new nose and a supporter below."

Clinton

A guest speaker told a class at the University of Arkansas, Fayetteville, that whether it's Lincoln, Churchill, or Hitler, all political leaders face an internal struggle between darkness and light. The darkness could be insecurity, depression, or family disorder. But in great leaders, the light overcomes the darkness though never without a struggle. These words were spoken by President William Clinton in 1981, after being voted out of office as Governor of Arkansas (Kiefer, 1998). As noted previously, Clinton has been a media focus since his first election as President in 1992. He and his wife have been investigated and reinvestigated by special counsels more than any other chief executive. Kiefer noted that politicians are often engaged in preemptive strikes fearing that someone, somewhere is a step away from attacking their good name and reputation. Clinton has apologized in several forums for his inappropriate behavior, and is engaged in pastoral counseling. His apologies only led to demands from the opposing political party to admit to further inappropriate and illegal acts. The media searchlight has examined the Clinton family behavior for many perspectives with stories that often exaggerate, embellish and utilize "spinning" to increase news sales.

Boedeker (1998) noted that the Clinton-Lewinsky story towered over the media landscape in 1998 with the unswerving ferocity of a monster on the rampage. Television administrators replayed the picture of Lewinsky and Clinton in an embrace repeatedly throughout the year.

The rise of cable news channels demonstrated how TV coverage has changed since Watergate. Boedeker continued by noting that commentary by legal analysts became repetitive theatre for the Lewinsky-Clinton affair, with hours of commentary including debate and conjecture about sex, politics, and perjury. Clinton who became adept at using the media together with public opinion polls for his communication and leadership skills, was caught in a dramatic tragedy. Major and minor characters crossed the television screen all zeroing in on detailed accounts of a consensual relationship between adults. The power of the media to make the news was demonstrated in the intensive, penetrating, ever-expanding focus on building the drama called *The White House in Crisis.* Media restraint was nowhere to be seen.

The Clinton saga reminds one of the English legal entanglements and excesses Charles Dickens (1868) depicted so well in *Bleak House.* Dickens wrote that some members of the High Court of Chancery bar are mistily engaged in one of the ten thousand precedents, groping knee-deep in technicalities, running their goat-hair and horse-hair warded heads against walls of words and making a pretence of equity with serious faces, as players might.

> ....The various solicitors in the cause....ranged in a line, in a long matted well (but you might look in vain for truth at the bottom of it) between the registrar's red table and the silk gowns with bills, cross-bills, answers, rejoinders, injunctions, affidavits, issues.... Mountains of costly nonsense, piled before them (Dickens: 2).

Dickens referred to a suit before the Court which was commenced nearly twenty years ago, with costs of over seventy thousand pounds, now no nearer to settlement than when it was begun (Dickens, xxvi). The lawsuit over wills destroyed the reputations of many innocent individuals along the way.

Throughout the Clinton impeachment hearings in both houses of Congress, there were repeated calls for following the letter of the law as revealed in the Constitution. One may note that the composition of the framers of the Constitution, most wealthy politically powerful men, did not reflect the actual population's diversity—women, ethnic groups, race, physically challenged, the working class, during their time or ours. The framers of the Constitution provided a system of checks and balances between the executive, legislative, and judicial branches of government that has stood the test of time. The founding fathers created a document that reflected the fact that the framers of the Constitution were as we are, prisoners of the age in which they lived. The ever-smaller number of voters participating in democratic elections often lead to governance by powerful ideological groups not representative of the nation's population.

Thus, as paradigm shifts occurred within the United States as the nation moved from an agrarian to an industrial to a post-industrial, to an information society a liberal, flexible not literal interpretation of the Constitution was more appropriate to meet the changing needs of an emerging new century. The nation's founders could not envision the power of media communications to influence elections, legislative decisions, or ad hominem attacks on public officials. The twenty-four hour or shorter news cycles replaced our founders' reasoned and thoughtful deliberations and compromises at the dawn of a new century.

Reasonable people engaged in arguments on both sides of the impeachment issue in a seriously divided and fragmented nation, as individuals and parties sought to play to television audiences (Grier, 1998). Partisanship predominated in the House of Representatives and the Senate as the debate evolved during 1998, 1999 and well into 2000.

President William Clinton, irked by New York Times columnist William Safire's conclusion that Hillary Rodham Clinton was a "congenital liar," stated that if he were not president he would have delivered a more forceful response to the bridge of Mr. Safire's nose. Clinton noted that presidents have feelings, too (Moffett 1996). Clinton who came from small town America with a difficult family background, and little financial means, was one of the lowest paid governors in the country with an annual salary of $36,000 a year. He relates to the needs and concerns of the nation's minorities and workforce poor and working classes. Clinton has incurred legal costs of over $5 million to defend himself from a series of sexual harassment, real estate, and other lawsuits (most of them dismissed). Seldom in the history of our Republic has there been such a lengthy and concerted effort to investigate anyone, let alone a second term elected president. Such investigatory zeal will have unforeseen multiplier effects in the future. Over time, the electorate has moved toward increased distrust and cynicism regarding public officials' pronouncements and actions. The press has become more adversarial in its relations with pronouncement of government officials at every level, especially since the Vietnam War.

Journalistic zeal often leads to credibility issues. Examples abound of journalists fabricating stories to enhance their careers. Badash (1993) notes a journalist ascribed an explosion in Port Chicago, California, to a nuclear weapon. Such spectacular claims are too often outright falsehoods, but the push to get a story, to increase sales of newspapers and television stories, often motivates young journalists to take a bridge too far—to fabricate stories, to build on spinning, hyperbole, and half-truths. Roser and Thompson (1995) examine the process by which fear transforms low-involvement audiences into active publics. They analyzed cognitive and emotional responses of uninvolved viewers to a film on environmental contamination, together with coping strategies to deal with the threat. Currently Congresspersons and the President use fear to gain votes for upcoming elections. On one side, individuals stress the danger to the elderly, young, disabled, minorities if government financed programs are cut or future expenditures reduced, while the other side focuses on the danger to future generations if there is not an attempt to reduce our nation's commitment to deficit spending for over half a century. Formerly uninvolved citizens on both sides of the issue have become actively involved by letting their government officials know of their fears. Wicks and Kern (1995) find that citizens seem to be getting more of their political information from paid advertisements. They also suggest new technologies might be used in innovative ways during election seasons.

An emerging phenomena is hate messages, distortions, mean spirited ad campaigns that predominate in election seasons. A record number of Congresspersons are leaving their jobs this year. As of March, 1996, some forty-one members (26 Democrats) of the House of Representatives and thirteen Senators (8 Democrats) left Congress. This is the largest exodus in history. Many report the increased lack of civility in politics and the fact that opponents with repeated one minute sound bites over a period of time can destroy anyone's reputation causing irreparable harm. Resigning Congresspersons stress the lack of compromise and extremists who are not willing to listen to other points of view as making governmental service no longer a happy experience. Not since 1896, when 12 senators retired, have so many seats in that chamber been open (1995).

Lehrer (1998) in a speech given at the International Center for Journalists' first annual Excellence in International Journalism, stated that polls rate journalists poorly. The reason for these low ratings, Lehrer found include:

- A new savagery that has become part and parcel of so-called new journalism. It is marked by predatory stakeouts, brutally coarse invasions of privacy, talk show shouting and violence, no-source reporting and other techniques.
- A new arrogance—words, sneers, and body language that say loud and clear: only journalists of America are pure enough to judge all others.
- A focus on entertainment with an expectation of fascinating reporting which will shorten a journalist career. Nobody can be fascinating for long, but people can be accurate and responsible for an entire career.
- Confusing personnel moves. News events often spawn new celebrities, actors, comedians, politicians, lawyers, infamous criminals now regularly masquerade as reporters. Examples include Watergate burglar G. Gordon Liddy and Clinton White House adviser George Stephanopoulos, both now widely considered to be journalists. Many administrators of news organizations fail to see any difference between real news and celebrity news. Individuals in charge of news organizations ought to value the vital importance of the responsibility to protect and preserve the values of real journalism.
- A blurring of lines among straight reporting, analysis and opinion, lead to a confused public. The public sees network reporters on the nightly news and then on weekends as commentators or pundits.
- On the print side, the public sees editors of weekly public affairs magazines, whose jobs are to direct even-handed coverage, writing stridently opinionated columns in newspapers and other publications about stories their own publications are covering.

Jim Lehrer finds new journalists might have seen him as an outdated, outmoded dinosaur for his efforts to promulgate responsible, ethical, journalism. He concludes by finding that those who practice, permit and encourage the new journalism, have an obligation to explain what they are doing and why. Failure to do so will continue to threaten the credibility and esteem of journalism (Lehrer, 1998).

Watson (1998) believes that reporters make an effort to provide
balanced information about conflicts in education. She sees a reporter's
job is to write about the issues without taking a side. When the media
do it right, they can help readers and viewers understand what is at
stake and explain the arguments about educational issues and
controversies. Watson writes that the media must take care, however,
not to get caught up in the enthusiasm that educators have for the latest
fad or in the ideology of the critics.

Good newspapers keep editorial writers and commentators separate
from news sections. Editorial writers tell readers what they should think
while reporters give them the information to make up their minds.
News research suggests that the public focuses on negative news about
public schools rather than positive reports. Watson illustrates the point
by noting a case of a newspaper that focused on two school projects in
1996. One was on the local district's efforts to get parent volunteers in
schools. The other was on lunchtime violence in schools. Both news
accounts got equal coverage with considerable time spent on the
stories, but while the cafeteria violence got a large public response with
parents, teachers, and students calling afterward with tips and ideas
about dealing with violence. The efforts on volunteering received little
attention from the public.

Watson concluded her article by noting that education reporters
regardless of criticism of fairness and balance in their reports must keep
their minds open, their eyes peeled for good stories, and their judgment
unclouded by ideology. Their job is to tell the truth and help readers
understand the challenges that society is facing and the truth may be
unpleasant. Reporters covering educational stories are too often
criticized emphasizing the negative about schools, while they are
reporting facts. The public tends to be more interested and attracted by
scandals, violence, and other dramatic incidences in schools.

Marks (1998) noted that newspapers' credibility has been declining
steadily along with circulation over the past 10 years. The nation's
editors were determined to address the issue of credibility. As part of
that effort, *The American Society of Newspaper Editors* released in late
1998 the findings of the first national survey on newspaper credibility.
The survey, part of a three-year study to understand and design
experimental programs to improve news reporting, was designed to
find the causes of journalists' disconnect with the public. Findings
included:

- A belief that newspapers don't show enough respect for, and knowledge of their readers and communities. A perception that newsprint stories are not accurate and run stories without checking them because they are printed in other newspapers.
- A suspicion that bias influences which stories are covered and how they are reported.
- Concern that sensational stories are covered only in an effort to sell newspapers.

Marks concluded by noting that media experts believe the print press can reestablish its credibility with the American public and national survey efforts can help focus on those problems that need correcting.

Smilliee (1998) noted that there is a growing industry of media watchers that encourage the news industry to do more reporting on itself. A $3 million dollar grant from the Philadelphia based *Pew Charitable Trusts* has been provided for conducting intensive polling on press performance as part of a Project for Excellence in Journalism while the Freedom Forum has provided $1 million on a study Free Press/Fair Press. Smilliee and Barringer (1998) noted that there has been a string of embarrassing media incidents including an internal investigation by First Amendment lawyer Floyd Abrams, which led to a CNN retracting of a story alleging U.S. forces dropped nerve gas in Vietnam. Writers at the Boston Globe and New Republic were fired for fabrications, while the Cincinnati Inquirer agreed to pay $10 million to Chiquita Brands International for theft of corporate voice-mail messages by a reporter. Bauder (1998) noted that CBS's "60 Minutes" apologized for reporting that Colombia's Cali drug cartel had opened a new heroin smuggling route to London. Investigators found producers of the program had faked locations and paid actors to portray drug couriers. These are just a few examples of unethical journalistic practices. In the 21st century, increased journalistic accuracy, integrity and morality will continue to be sought.

Films and Perceptions of History

Currently the film industry continues its snapshots of historical events as witness *Dr. Strangelove* in 1964, *The Grapes of Wrath* in 1940, *Mississippi Burning* in 1988, *All the President's Men* in 1976, and the current *Nixon* in 1995. Winkler (1995) citing historical scholars notes many of these films create a serious distortion of history. Taking liberties as artists, film directors set tones, moods, and character flaws to stimulate audience attendance at showings. As Winkler (1995) notes there is a sense in which filmmakers blend fantasy and reality. Boedeker (2000) found *Public Broadcasting System* ambitious portrayal of 41 U.S. chief executives appeared to be a throwback to anecdote-packed texts where personality upstages policy. PBS's full-fledged presidential biographies provide more in-depth analysis of the role of chief executives. Even these in-depth biographies, however, often blend fact and fiction due to time constraints as well as the need for broad audience appeal.

Historians are becoming more interested in studying popular culture through film documentaries as well as feature films, since they reach a wider audience and give them an opportunity to correct discrepancies in their teaching and writing according to Winkler. He finds most historians agree that there are a lot of questions to be explored in reference to perceptions of history through films.

1. Do films over-emphasize individuals and actions? Often long-term socio-economic trends may be played down.
2. How does the history of a film influence the history that it portrays? Serious scholars of the subject need to pay more attention to who financed a film and how it was produced. This would be applicable to a recent documentary on Newt Gringrich of Georgia which depicted him in a slanted public broadcasting film.
3. Can films deal with complexity? Often a film sends a message that things are getting better or worse. How does one judge that?
4. How much should films invent the past? Many are critical of films like Oliver Stone's *JFK* and others like *Nixon* which paints a picture with little grounding in fact. The *Nixon* film sets a mood of darkness, swearing, and drinking which is contrary to the facts according to those who worked with him.

Since historical films are becoming more prevalent, the question of standards of content accuracy needs to be examined. The film industry often sends a social political message through its portrayal of events. In a society seeking a quick, cheap technological fix to complex problems, single-issue films encourage anti-intellectualism, dogmatism, and inaccurate reporting of facts. It is important to encourage our students to question accuracy of all forms of media reporting.

The role of the 4th estate (mass media) as an independent and powerful force in society is an enduring and controversial issue (1995). Understanding information and communication policy as power is important in today's environment since there has been a qualitative shift in the level of dependence upon information technologies and in the degree to which activities are informational (Braman,1993). The use of new information technologies permits the state like other institutions and cultural forms, to evolve. A new form of state is emerging, specializing in forms of power specific to the environment of global telecommunication networks (Braman, 1995).

Technological Addiction

Increasingly individuals seek to keep up with the latest innovations in technology. Advances in computer technology require updating every six months to a year to keep current and to be able to use the latest software that requires ever-more powerful hardware. The industry has built in obsolence that makes it difficult for business and educational institutions to keep up with the latest hardware and software requirements.

Not only do we have an increase in the population addicted to computer updating, but currently with the World Wide Web and the Internet, researchers have found a growing problem with addiction to using computers. Marco R. Della Cava (1996) finds that in colleges, surfing the net has become a serious addiction. She reports on a number of universities whose counseling staffs are taking steps to deal with the growing problem. At the University of Maryland staff psychologist Linda Tipton finds scholarship students with Internet addictions are flunking out of school. At the University of Texas at Austin, counselor Linda Morgan Bost reported on an undergraduate student who, when denied a modem by her parents, supplemented the prescribed 11 hours a day on campus terminals with time on a friend's. Della Cava reports on International Development Council research showing some 89.1 million people use the Internet and a third of them have Web access. IDC reports an estimated 199 million will be on-line in 1999, with 62% of them on the Web. She notes that college students are particularly at risk since universities give them no-cost linkage. The Counseling Center at the University of Maryland has a "Caught in the Net" group session for students to attend weekly.

The University of Washington keeps abuse in check by metering Internet access to its students. At the University of Texas, Bost plans a low-key marketing technique to encourage those kids who have gone well beyond the infatuation phase. At Michigan State psychologists are on the lookout for Internet overuse that is viewed as similar to alcoholism and drug abuse. Della Cava relates the research on Internet abusers and their families by Kimberly S. Young, a University of Pittsburgh Professor. Young who started her work after a friend called in tears saying her husband was addicted to America Online, using it 40 hours a week and running up huge telephone bills.

The Internet addiction syndrome is too new for psychologists to understand. Some feel it is better for students to overuse, overwork on the net than for them to engage in more hazardous activities such as violence, vandalism, drug abuse, or other forms of detrimental behavior. One observing individuals in their offices at any major university may well find that faculty and staff are following the same pattern as their students, and spending hours on the World Wide Web working with Netscape or other browsers. Older citizens and others who are addicted to the web, have physical symptoms including neck, arm, back, and vision problems.

Virtual romance on Internet is of increased interest to psychologists and counselors. In some instances, divorce cases have been filed over the content of e-mail messages given to spouses. A case recently involved an e-mail message sent to a woman and signed "The Weasel." The husband found a message addressed to his wife "I gotta tell you that I am one happy guy now and so much at peace again anticipating us. I love you dearly. XXOOXX". The husband filed for divorce and is seeking custody of the couple's two children. He claimed the pair planned a real tryst at a New Hampshire bed-and-breakfast inn (1996). Peterson and Miller (1996) find that infidelity is rampant on the Internet. Legal fallout has now reached the courtroom. They noted that the Catholic Church position is that such lustful virtual affairs are a sin. In some cases these intense relationships can become addictive because of immediate feedback; some participants spend more hours on the Internet than with their spouses. But others wonder if it's really a matter of infidelity or just a matter of "mousing" around. Excessive computer use may also represent loneliness or lack of human contact. Some families own several computers and e-mail each other within their own homes about daily events as "what's for supper?" rather than engaging in face to face interaction.

Popular culture is reflected on the Internet through increased access to films, music, and literature. Particularly worrisome to educators and parents is the influence pornography, easily accessed on Internet, will have on America's youth. Efforts to deal with the issue overtime are seen in three major legislative acts. First, *The Communications Act of 1934* which established that airways are public property, commercial broadcasters are to be licensed to use the airways and the main condition for use is whether the broadcaster served the public interest, convenience and necessity. Second, was the *Children's Television Act of 1990* reaffirmed the need for broadcasters to serve the public interest, convenience and necessity. It also affirmed that television broadcasters must serve the educational and informational needs of children and will not have their broadcast licenses renewed if they fail to meet the needs of children.

Although much of this law remains to be developed because FCC has not established guidelines for the educational and informational needs of children, it served to encourage debate (1996). Third, the *Telecommunications Act of 1996* included provisions for *Communications Decency* which made it a crime to put indecent materials on interactive computer services where minors might find them, required a 'V-chip' in television sets to help parents control what children might see and authorized a television rating (1996). In a rapidly expanding global information highway, it is difficult to keep up with ever-growing communication networks. A decision of a panel of federal judges for the U.S. District Court in Philadelphia on June 12, 1996 overturned the *Communication Decency Act* which was part of the 1996 *Telecommunications Act.* The rationale behind the decision was identified by U.S. District Judge Steward Dalzell, who stated that any content-based regulation of the Internet, no matter how benign the purpose, could burn the global village to roast the pig. He continued by noting that the Internet may be fairly regarded as a never-ending worldwide conversation. The government may not, through the *Communications Decency Act*, interrupt that conversation. As the most participatory form of mass speech yet developed, the Internet deserves the highest protection from governmental intrusion (1996).

Although there will be appeals to the Supreme Court on the basis parents can be assisted in protecting children from sexually explicit material on the Internet, the Philadelphia District Court judges stressed the *Decency Act* unconstitutional and that the First Amendment denies Congress the power to regulate protected speech on the Internet. It is clear that 21st century technology is increasing the complexity of monitoring the media. Federal courts have consistently affirmed the value and importance of the first amendment freedom of speech rights throughout history as the epitome of a pluralistic democratic society. There has been continuing debate since Plato's time over what children should be permitted to read and see.

Media and Demagoguery

Anti-intellectualism is alive and well in America in the 21st century. Distrust of intellectuals has a long history. John Locke placed "book learning" in fourth or last place in his hierarchy of values. Mark Twain found soap and schooling are not as sudden as a massacre, but are more deadly in the long run. Margaret Mead noted that her grandmother wanted her to get an education so she kept her out of school. Ralph Waldo Emerson in a response to Horace Mann's lecture in 1839 crusading for the public school, said that we are shut in schools for ten or fifteen years, and come out at last with a bellyful of words and do not know a thing (1975). Former Governor George Wallace of Alabama referred to pointy headed intellectuals.

Seib (1995) discusses how the Republicans could win a big battle over the budget but possibly lose in coming elections due in part to demagoguery which works with American voters. He points to the fact that the difference in Medicare spending is minuscule by both parties, yet Clinton and Gore's constant repeated rhetoric of potential devastation of the proposed Republican budget for the elderly, poor, minorities and disabled have sunk in for voters. Fortunately compromise and cooperation ended in a workable budget for 2000. The one-minute, television oft repeated television soundbites can, and do, shape elections and public policy. Both parties utilize hasty generalization, overgeneralization, and appeal to the masses to sell their agenda. Behind these actions are Madison Avenue public relations experts in the psychology of human manipulation advising leaders in both parties as to the best way to get a message across. Increasingly mean-spiritedness, hate language, and half-truths are taking center stage in American politics.

Cortes (1995) noted that media impact varies among readers, viewers, and listeners, with race and ethnicity of recipients often playing a significant role in media-audience learning relationships. He found that schools need to assess the impact of media to strengthen multicultural educational pedagogy and curricula. Treatment of individuals from diverse cultural backgrounds in films, television and the press needs to be studied, particularly from the perspective of popular culture and conflict resolution.

Cooper (1986) finds that children remember advertising slogans better than memorized facts from school, and the media instills in them inaccurate views of the world. Cooper suggests that parents must stress the unreal nature of television programs and advertisements, and replace them with the value of ethics that includes enabling individuals to think, know, express and act for themselves. Luke and Myers (1995) find children who are exposed to violence in media and everyday life may choose aggression as a means to solve problems.

Marks (1996, January) notes that news media and the press is slicker, more sensational, cyclical, opinionated, and celebrity driven than before. He finds public respect at a low level and cites increased studies about media trends including Howard Kurtz's *Hot Air: All Talk All the Time,* James Fallows' *Breaking the News: How the Media Undermine American Democracy* and Drobert Lichter, co-author of *Good Intentions Make Bad News.* There is a intertwining of the establishment press and sensational tabloids that needs to be dealt with by better monitoring by media and press themselves. Media personalities often make the news rather than interpret events and decisions based on as much factual evidence as possible. Marks (1996, February) reports on a $1.5 million National Television Violence Study released February 8, 1996. The study financed by the cable industry as a response to public outcries over programming content revealed violence in most of the 2,500 hours of programs analyzed. Punching, slapping, kicking, shootings were commonplace with perpetrators of violence going unpunished in 73 percent of all violent scenes. The study has led individuals to explore ways of dealing with the issue of TV violence. The 1996 Telecommunications Reform Bill, signed into law by

President Clinton requires the entertainment industry to set up a rating system. In addition, television manufacturers are required to install a computer chip, the V-chip, which will allow parents to screen out violent programs.

MTV and other popular youth programs may be forms of anti-establishment protests. Frequently we have news accounts of youth violence on property and persons that follow violent television or film scripts as individuals act them out in real life. Thus in addition to the Telecommunications Reform Bill, efforts will be made to create safe harbors by channeling violent programming into hours when children don't make up a substantial part of the audience according to Marks.

Ledell (1995) notes that educators have a duty to assist students in understanding that we must be tolerant of many points of view without becoming divided. She notes we must help students examine political and religious issues without proselytizing, and help them move from antagonism and intolerance to civility.

The Future

Popular culture invading us through electronics, soundbites and sound enhancement devices is part of the face of 21st century America. We can learn a great deal from low culture through realistic messages, common person language usage, dissemination of personal narrative or search for meaning in a world perceived as insecure. From the perspective of the increased power of media to utilize emotions, half-truths, disinformation, misinformation, hate language, destructive one-minute soundbites to sell a point of view or a product, it is timely to consider encouraging individuals to learn to question, to analyze, to think critically, to become involved in making a difference in one's society and world. We may become a nation of couch potatoes, tolerating violence and degradation against persons in films as in real life. The fourth estate has done many things to improve our society, but it is essential to monitor media ethics through professional journalistic associations and the reading and viewing public.

Orwell, cited in Hapgood (1974) cautioned us to read people's intentions by their use of language. He noted that if the words are long and so fuzzy that we cannot understand what is being said, or if we surmise they are saying nothing at all, we can be fairly sure the speaker is trying to swindle us. In politics as in advertising, Arthur Herzog drew a distinction between lying and faking. He found a lie is something you get caught at, while a fake is fail-safe. A fake is a statement, that while designed to deceive, is too mushy and impenetrable to get you into trouble; no one can disprove a fake (your car warranty) for example because no one can figure out exactly what it is saying. Hapgood mentioned "wordnoise" as use of language to sell a point of view regardless of its veracity. Currently governmental leaders use policy wonk to disseminate information to the public. The media uses this wonk (double-talk-bureaucratic discourse) to stimulate interest in their audience.

McLuhan (1967) illustrates the power of the media to change the society. As he notes we cannot return to the past, new technology is moving our society, our world into new frontiers, new interfaces, new opportunities. He wrote that the medium, or process, of our time—electronic technology—is reshaping and restructuring patterns of social interdependence and every aspect of our personal life. He finds it is forcing us to reconsider and reevaluate practically every thought, every action and every institution. McLuhan correctly notes that politics offers yesterday's answers to today's questions. A new politics is emerging where living rooms have become voting booths as participation via television is changing everything. Naisbitt (1994) finds our telecommunications revolution will empower individuals as never before with more access to information, greater speed in execution and greater ability to network with more people in more places. Naisbitt notes that new scrutiny of politicians and political activity is increasing around the world and where standards of decency and ethical conduct are found wanting the public is demanding retribution. The public increasingly uses chat rooms, web sites, news groups and on-line political action groups.

Reeves (1996) found that more than half of political advertising now is negative for the reason that it is effective—it sells. Reeves reports on the findings of Shanto Iyengar of UCLA and Stephen Ansolbehere of MIT who report that people making political commercials are not only fooling the public, but making fools of the press. Iyengar and Ansolbehere suggest in their book *Going Negative* that negativity wins in campaign reporting and the press cannot stop it. They surveyed CNN stories which repeated the theme of the advertisements several times, often replaying the relevant segments from the advertisements. By repeating the advertisement itself, recall is strengthened and favorable information about the candidate and unfavorable information about the opponent are more accessible in memory.

Charles Frankel wrote *Democratic Prospect* in 1962. His foresight is evident in his analysis of the challenges of functioning in an open society. Frankel found that although open societies are our best hope for the future, cant, obscurantism, and lies are, of course, a good part of the diet of most democracies. Frankel found that the principle of freedom of the press or media was laid down when press was a means of individual expression, comment and criticism. Now it is an industry for profit, using techniques of mass suggestion and possessing great power.

He continued by noting that the slanting of news and information is one of the more obvious of the problems that have been aggravated by the rise of mass media; and another problem, whose existence is attested by the results of most national elections during the last thirty years, mass media does not fairly reflect the spectrum of opinions that actually exist in the community (1962). Frankel finds the most important issue is the influence of mass media on the shape and temperature of public opinion, on questions addressed, kinds of solutions looked for, and the atmosphere in which it is formed. He finds that the mass media, competing in the marketplace of commodities, not ideas, and trying to keep and trap the attention of great numbers of people who have other things on their minds, serve up a special kind of diet.

Frankel noted that the visceral, momentary, the odd take precedence because bad news is good news because it sells more stories. He continues by noting that the procession of human affairs is cut up into a series of shocks and crises, torn loose from their contexts, with only a brief past behind them and a melodramatic future ahead. The final result Frankel notes is the deformation of men's sense of the public world, the distortion of events and the misshaping of history.

Popular culture is reflected in our communications and global information exchanges. We, as educators, as citizens, have a moral and ethical obligation to assist in monitoring our mass media. As Jefferson noted that any nation which expects to be ignorant and free, expects what never was and never will be. Our individual and collective freedom in an open pluralistic society depends on the quality of the information on which citizens act. Governmental leaders at every level must not be chosen on a media attractive basis but on consideration of fitness to exercise reflective, responsible, decisive and independent decision making. Reputations should not be destroyed by repeated negative one-minute soundbites. Reputations destroyed by malicious media reports are very difficult to resurrect even when the information is proven inaccurate, incorrect and built on no factual basis. Use of negative and emotive overtones of language can sell newspapers but lead to use of hate language and action based on misinformation. Our best hope for the future is the use of education to alert citizens to the necessity of critically analyzing media information dissemination.

It is this author's opinion that no nation can withstand the onslaught of media disinformation, hasty generalization, mean spirited messages, or half-truths so prevalent in the last few years without some often unintended multiplier effects. Voter alienation, distrust, and disbelief in politician and government officials pronouncements may continue to result in low voter turnout. Thurman (1998) found that truth turns out to be fiction. Thurman reports that the Washington Post's Janet Cooke was stripped of a Pulitzer Prize when it was found that she made up a story about a drug child addict in 1981.

Thurman finds several causes for lack of integrity among journalists. First, there is a proliferation of media outlets with cable, the Internet, with reporters trying to stay atop the clutter. Second, ethics and standards are under siege as reporters do not take the time to check facts before press and airtime. Third, with pressures of competition leading to a frenzy kind of new coverage, shoddy work too often occurs, according to the former editor of the Chicago Tribune. Fourth, serious journalism is often overshadowed by scurrilous details of pseudo-celebrities like Monica Lewinsky, and celebrities like Diana, Princes of Wales. There is often a dearth of local news coverage. Fifth, news events are occurring so rapidly, retractions are often given but a momentary glance by the listening, viewing and reading public. News analysts are entertainers who use a variety of stimulating backdrops for their reports, or some are "news readers", not reporters.

Thurman lists several serious cases of malfeasance in journalism. The Cincinnati Enquirer has run three front page apologies to Chiquita Brands International and paid the firm over $10 million, over untrue conclusions about the company's employment and business practices which were based on unethically obtained information. Another case of irresponsible journalism was a joint report by Cable News Network and Time charging that the U.S. military used nerve gas against U.S. defectors during the Vietnam War. So gross has been the problem with ethical journalism that the *Committee of Concerned Journalists* now has over 1,000 reporter members, and conducted over a dozen forums with journalists nationwide.

Owen (1998) found radio firmly embedded in American 21st century culture. Radio talk shows have been a focus of anger, cynicism, and confrontation for over a decade. Individuals can participate yet maintain anonymity, spouting off about their feelings, biases, and prejudices with talk radio hosts of similar opinions. Although sensationalism, emotional rhetoric, vitriolic public discord has a history from colonial broadsheets that printed gossip and scandal used by our nation's founders, to the penny press period of the 1800s, "yellow journalism", "muckraking" and tabloid style reporting were part of the media of our past. Owen continued by noting that the intense edge, unbridled incivility, with verbal attacks on the nation's leaders, such as Bill Clinton's nicknames "Slick Willie" or "Sick Willie", is what makes the current forum different from the past. Owen, Professor of Government at Georgetown University, believes talk radio will continue to reflect an angry, alienated citizenry, more prone to perpetual belittling, complaints and spewing forth flames of venom and hate, than any meaningful attempt to improve society. Together with other communication avenues, radio talk show hosts have been instrumental in demeaning the nation's leaders.

Zeroing in on every national leader's action or behavior were fertile grounds for zinger cartoons, used to demean, criticize, and ridicule them. A few examples of such media denigration were: emphasizing Gerald Ford's trick knee which caused him to fall occasionally while getting off a plane, George Bush's throwing up on a Japanese premier while ill, Jimmy Carter using an oar to fight off rabbits attacking his boat, Lyndon Johnson's picking up his hound dogs by their ears, Nixon's depicting of a four o'clock shadow and "I am not a crook." Johnson's attacks during the Vietnamese War "how many kids have you killed today?" Playing to the pernicious side of the public, media focuses on controversy and scandal that has led to an era of distrust, fragmentation, alienation, and scorched earth policy politics.

Chomsky (1997) discussed the use of media information control by the military and the government. Use of propaganda techniques to influence public opinion has been part of the American historical landscape. Chomsky traced the history of propaganda noting the Creel Commission appointed by Woodrow Wilson, was used to turn a pacifistic population into raving hysterics who wanted to destroy everything German to save ourselves from Huns who were tearing the arms off Belgian babies. Lies and disinformation continue to be part of our media communication networks, partially due to information control. Swings of public opinion were noted in a move from support of Saddam Hussein during the Iranian-Iraq War to viewing him as a ruthless dictator during and after the Iraq-Kuwaiti War as well as from support for Panama leader Manuel Noriega to vilifying him as a thug, a narcotics-trafficker, and ruthless dictator. Chomsky continued by noting that often opportunities for peaceful resolution of world conflicts are ignored through misinformation or disinformation. Although there are varying evaluations of Chomsky's *Media Control*, propaganda has been repeatedly used to justify military action in the global community. Chechen's wonder why Western Nations were quick to respond to Serbia's maltreatment of Kosovos by round-the-clock military action, while no such response has occurred in their plight with thousands upon thousands of refugees. Media reporting of the Kosovo plight might be seen as more intense and persistent than with the Chechens displacement.

How can we effectively make a difference in the quality of our information systems on which decisions about the quality of life for the future of the individual and society depend? Walker (1994) interviewed Walter Cronkite recently. Cronkite noted that there has been a general deterioration of journalistic standards in all areas, print as well as broadcasting, in the sense that media currently indulge in covering stories that in the past would be ignored by serious journalistic organs. Cronkite found a "tabloidization" of journalism, because sensationalism sells, and attention spans are so short it takes a spectacular episode to bring attention back to a central theme. Cronkite found a superficiality in both the media and the public, each feeding each other's touch-and-go outlook on the world. There is a lot of information but not a lot of understanding. He noted that we are almost being overcommunicated at, not communicated with.

Nonetheless Supreme Court Justice Hugo Black, often considered one of the two most important justices in American History, although haunted and pained by his former membership in the KKK, was a committed liberal who noted that only a free and unrestrained press can effectively expose deception in government (1995).

Press freedoms have First Amendment protections that raised important questions in our super-information highway and network age. The current global community could not have been foreseen over two centuries ago. In 1790 the United States population was four million when it was decided that Congress shall make no law....abridging the freedom of speech or the press. There was little if any discussion about possible limits of First Amendment freedoms.

In 1999 the concept is less clear. The First Amendment does not define the precise nature of freedom or identify clearly who is to enjoy the right of free speech and the press. Does an individual have restrictions on his or her right to yell fire in a crowded theater for fun? (1991). The rights of editors and publishers to express themselves must be associated with the right of the public to be served with a substantial and honest basis of fact for its judgments on events (Hutchins, 1947).

Heller (1996) discusses the work of Robert D. Putnam, a professor of government and international affairs at Harvard addressing an ever-dwindling sense of community in the United States. This tendency to avoid joining groups of any kind might be due to a widespread distrust of political or other institutions. Putnam finds Americans turning inward and suspicious. He finds a possible cause of 'civil disengagement' is television that takes more time from people interaction and takes an increasing amount of an individuals time. Passive rather than active participation is becoming the norm as more time is spent as an observer on the human scene.

Stuller (1996) discusses the social effect of a technological age with an increasing number of individuals communicating through computer Internets, cellular phones, pagers, pocket computers, radio equipped modems at work, at home, on vacation and driving to and from work. Many auto accidents are caused by individuals reaching for cellular phones and not paying attention to their driving. As Putnam noted, Stuller finds the age of automation in all its forms together with fear of crime are increasingly robbing individuals of an opportunity for social contact. Lots of young people today refer to the computer with its second generation DVD multimedia systems as their best friends, which may lead to a silent, anonymous epidemic of shyness, according to Stuller. It will be increasingly interesting to explore the phenomenon of isolation and turning inward in American life created, at least in part, by technology.

It is clear that our information sources are in the hands of fewer and fewer major corporations as mergers, takeovers and buyouts decrease the number of independent media organizations. Television news magazines use audience research to track public preferences on a minute-by-minute basis. Editorial judgment is shaped by demographics and ratings research. Getting a big interview with folks in the news spotlight such as Monica Lewinsky produces ratings that build up the financial bottom line. Finding breaking news stories is a key mission of news magazine programs.

We must continue to find ways to monitor the media to assure a high quality of journalism. Scholars need to be engaged in addressing and identifying the ramifications of a technological age in which schools at all levels, businesses in all fields, and all of the nation's governmental functions are encouraging the use of the latest technology to speed dissemination and access of information. There must be a continuing effort to the value of placing all media systems in proper perspective as a tool to improve the quality of human life, rather than an end in itself. More funds in many instances are currently going into media hardware and software rather than into other essentials in education.

The quality of a civilization depends on mutual respect for the dignity and worth of individuals. This respect is best represented by media organizations thoroughly committed to the highest sense of responsible journalism—essential for a democratic society to operate effectively and fully in theory and practice with an informed citizenry.

References

Akst, Daniel (1998, December 18). "The Future of the Book". *The Wall Street Journal*: W 15.

Associated Press (1996, January 11). "Clinton's Spat With Press Has Its Precedents", *Christian Science Monitor:* 4.

Badash, Lawrence and Hewlett, Richard D. (June 1993). "A Story Too Good to Kill: The 'Nuclear' Explosion in San Francisco Bay", *Knowledge: Creation, Diffusion, and Utilization.* Vol. 14, No: 356-371.

Balz, Dan (1998, December 18). "Partisan Political Debate Eats Away at Washington". *Sun-Sentinel*: 22 A.

Barringer, Felicity (1998, July 4). "Ex-CNN Producer: Story True". *Sun-Sentinel*: 3 A.

Bauder, David (1998, December 12). "Faked Documentary". *Tulsa World:* D 5.

Boedeker, Hal (1998, December 28). "All Monica, All The Time". *The Orlando Sentinel:* G 10.

Boedeker, Hall (2000, April 8). "PBS Examines Quirks of all the Presidents". *Sun Sentinel, South Florida*: 3D.

Bok Sissela (1978). *Lying: Moral Choice in Public and Private Life.* New York: Pantheon Books: 3-4.

Braman, Sandra (1993). "Harmonization of Systems", *Journal of Communication.* Vol. 45, No. 3: 133-140.

Braman, Sandra (1995, Autumn). "Horizons of the State: Information Policy and Power". *Journal of Communication.* Volume 45, No. 4: 4-24.

Campbell, Kim (2000, March 15). "Scene Set for a Reading Revolution". *The Christian Science Monitor*: 1, 4.

Chomsky, Noam (1997). *Media Control:* New York: Seven Stories Press: 46-58.

Clines, Francis X. (1998, December 18). "GOP Backs Livingston Despite Disclosure". *Sun-Sentinel:* 23A.

Cooper, Thomas (1986-1987, Fall-Winter). "Communication and Ethics: The Informal and Formal Curricula". *Journal of Mass Ethics.* Volume 2, No.1: 71-79.

Cortes, Carlos E. (1995). "Knowledge Construction and Popular Culture", in *Handbook of Research on Multicultural Education:* 169-183. UD 030 379 ED382705.

Della Cava, Marco R. (1996, January 16). "Are Heavy Users Hooked or Just On-Line Fanatics"? *USA Today:* 1A, 2A.

Dickens, Charles (1992). *Bleak House,* Original Publication 1852-1853. New York: Bantam House.

Donahue, George A., Tichenor, Phillip J. and Olien, Clarice N. (1995, Spring). "A Guard Dog Perspective on the Role of Media". *Journal of Communication.* Vol. 45, No.: 115-132.

Estrada, Richard (1998, December 22). "Truth Is Not Private Property to Use as We Wish: Take Prize from Author". *Sun-Sentinel:* 25 A. (1996, February 11). "Virtual Affair Lands Wife in Divorce Net". *Tulsa   World:* Classified, p. 16.

Feldmann, Linda (1998, December 22). "Two Views of U.S. Political Future". *The Christian Science Monitor:* 1, 9.

Fox, Arent (1996, June 13). "Telecommunications Act of 1996". *Arent Fox Communications Group:* 1,2 World Wide Web, Internet.

Frankel, Charles (1962). *Democratic Prospect.* New York: Harper and Row: 74-76.

Grier, Peter (1998, December 17). "Clinton's Collision with History: Impeachment Vote Divides Politicians...And Public...In Ways That Could Affect The Country For Years". *The Christian Science Monitor:* 1, 14.

Gross, Ronald and Beatrice (1975, March). "A Nation of Learners". *American Education:* 27.

Guelke, Adrian (1998, Fall). "Wars of Fear: Coming to Grips With Terrorism". *Harvard International Review:* 45-47.

Hapgood, David (1974). *The Screwing of the Average Man.* New York: Doubleday: 16-17.

Harwood, John and Cummins, Jeanne (1998, December 11). "Tactical Retreat: One Likely Casualty of the Clinton Years: The Scandal Gambit". *The Wall Street Journal:* 1, A 6.

Heller, Scott (1996, March 1). "Bowling Alone". *The Chronicle of Higher Education:* A10,12.

Holden, Stephen (1996, January 8,). "A Gadget-Mad America, Through Japanese Eyes". *The New York Times*: B2.

Holmstrom, David (1998, May 28). "Separating the Wheat from the Tares in News". *The Christian Science Monitor*: B 11.

Kaul, Donald (1998, July 4). "Firing a Few Writers Won't Restore Credibility". *Sun-Sentinel*: 15 A.

Lawrence, Jay (2000, January 31). "Media Mergers, Morphs, Mutation". *The Christian Science Monitor:* 9.

Kiefer, Francine (1998, December 17). "Clinton's Collision with History: From Private Struggles to Public Crisis". *The Christian Science Monitor*: 1,14.

Ledell, Marjorie (1995). *How to Avoid Crossfire and Seek Common Ground: a Journey for the Sake of Children.* Arlington, Virginia: American Association of School Administrators.

Lehrer, Jim (1998, October 16). "Journalism on the Precipice". *The Christian Science Monitor:* 15.

Luke, Jennifer L. and Myers, Catherine (1995, Winter). "Toward Peace: Using Literature to Aid Conflict Resolution". *Childhood Education.* Volume 71, No 2: 66-69.

Marks, Alexandra (1996, January 30, Tuesday). "Media Insiders Give Profession Low Marks". *Christian Science Monitor:* 1,13.

Marks, Alexandra (1996, February 8). "Study 'Pulls No Punches' About Television Violence". *Christian Science Monitor:* 3.

Marks, Alexandra (1998, December 16). "To Public, The Press Often Gets It Wrong". *The Christian Science Monitor:* 2.

McLuhan, Marshall (1967). *The Medium is the Massage-Message.* New York: Bantam Books: 1, and (1965) *Understanding The Extension of Man.* New York: McGraw Hill.

Hutchins, Robert M. (1947). "What Can Be Done" in *A Free and Responsible Press.* Chicago: University of Chicago Press: 27, 81, 96, 99.

Moffett, George (1996, January 11). "How Media Blitz Alters Peacekeeping Missions". *Christian Science Monitor.* Volume 88, No.27: 1,5.

Morgenstern, Joe (1998, December 18). "In 'You've Got Mail', Cyber-Love Conquers All, Even a Predictable Script". *The Wall Street Journal*: W 1.

Naisbitt, John (1994). *Global Paradox.* New York: Avon Books: 128.

Neal, Ken (1998, December 13). "The Johnson Model". *Tulsa World:* G 6.

Newcomb, Amelia (1998, October 27). "Shaking Things Up". *The Christian Science Monitor:* B 1.

Owen, Diana (1998, November 16). "Talk Radio's Price: A Culture of Complaint". *The Christian Science Monitor*: 13.

Page, Clarence (1998, December 24). "Larry Flynt Sets Agenda For Congress". *Sun-Sentinel*: 13 A.

Parker, Suzi (1998, October 27). "In Ever-Changing Workplace: Two-Year Colleges Fill Niche". *The Christian Science Monitor:* 3.

Peterson, Karen S. and Miller, Leslie (1996, February 6). "Cyberflings Are Heating up the Internet". *USA Today:* Section D 1.

Ravitch, Diane (1998, December 17). "Girls Are Beneficiaries of Gender Gap". *The Wall Street Journal*: A 22.

Reeves, Richard (1996, January 24, Wednesday). "The Dirty Business of Politics". *Tulsa World:* A7.

Roser, Connie and Thompson, Margaret (1995, Winter). "Fear Appeals and the Formation of Active Publics", *Journal of Communication:* Vol. 45, No. 1: 103-121.

Rothstein, Edward (1995, January 8). "Connections: Cyborgs 'r' (Almost) Us, or How We May be Turning into a Multimedia Experience". *New York Times*: C3.

Sandberg, Jared (1996, June 13). "Federal Judges Block Censorship on the Internet". *Wall Street Journal:* B1, B5. (1995, December 2, Saturday). "Hatfield will Retire; Simpson Also May Quit". *Tulsa World:* News 5.

Slambrouck, Paul Van (2000, April 5). "A Monopoly Game With New Rules". *The Christian Science Monitor*: 1, 5.

Seib, Gerald F. (1995, December 13). "Could the GOP Win A Big Battle But Lose the War"? *Wall Street Journal:* A 20.

Sheppard, Judy (1995 Saturday, February 11). "From Kluxer to No. 1 Liberal". *The Atlanta Journal-The Atlanta Constitution:* A3.

Smillie, Dirk (1998, August 20). " Media's Own *Mea Culpas* Lead to More Self-Scrutiny". *The Christian Science Monitor*: B 3.

Stuller, Jan (1996, March). "The Connected". *Kiwanis Magazine:* 28-31. "Three Telecommunications Laws: Their Impact and Significance". (1996, June 13,). San Francisco, California: *Center for Educational Priorities*: 1,2.Internet WWW.

Thurman, James J. (1998, July 3). "News Integrity: Get It Right vs. Make a Splash". *The Christian Science Monitor:* 1,14.

Thurman, James J. (1998, November 30). "Campaign to Paint Starr in Warmer Colors May Be Paying Off". *The Christian Science Monitor:*3.

Toffler, Alvin and Toffler, Heidi (1998 June-July). "Preparing for Conflict in the Information Age". *The Futurist:* 26-29.

Toy, Vivian S. (1996, January 8). "Valone Offers Plan for Schools". *New York Times:* B12.

Van Atta, Dale (1998, Fall). "Carbombs and Cameras". *Harvard International Review:* 66-70.

Van Patten, James (1991, Fall,). "Multi-Media Communications and Democracy". *Journal of Thought:* Volume 26, Nos. 3 and 4: 18-30.

Walker, Sam (1994, March 7). "Cronkite on the Changing Media". *Christian Science Monitor:* 16.

Walsh, Mark (1998, October 28). "Schools Can't Ban Books Because of Complaints, Court Says". *Education Week:* 5.

Ware, Robert Bruce and Straus (2000, March 19). "Media Bias on Chechnya". *Christian Science Monitor:* 11.

Watson, Aleta (1998, June). "The Newspaper's Responsibility". *Phi Delta Kappan:* 729-754.

Weinberg, Steve (1998, October 22). "Two Objective Looks at Objectivity". *The Christian Science Monitor:* B 9.

Wicks, Robert H. and Kern, Montague (1995, April). "Factors Influencing Decisions by Local Television News Directors to Develop New Reporting Strategies During the 1992 Campaign". *Communication Research.* Volume 22, No. 2: 237-255.

Winkler, Karen J. (1995, December 15). "History in Hollywood: The Way Films Present the Past". *The Chronicle of Higher Education:* A10- A 16.

Conclusion—The Future

There are similarities between our times and those at the turn of the 20th century. Then and now multiple forces challenged the status quo. Massive movements of peoples from have-not to have nations occurred resulting in stereotyping, fear and intolerance. Over a million newcomers to America from 1890s through the early 1900s changed the demographics of the United States. The same trend continues in our 21st century as thousands of third-world citizens emigrate to industrialized societies in Europe and the United States. International upheaval permeated the world stage in the early 20th century. The Austrian-Hungarian Empire was breaking up, Asia was in turmoil, Europe was in disarray with Germany on the verge of war preparation. At the turn of the 21st century Kosovo refugees have returned to their ravaged homes while the "Balkanization" of the region continues to challenge NATO and the United Nations. Regional violence in Kosovo, Serbia, Chechnya, Indonesia, India, Pakistan, Israel, Arabia and elsewhere continues to plague efforts toward world peace. At the turn of the 20th century there was an intellectual ferment in America. Leading writers, "muckrakers" were challenging big business ethics, corruption, labor sweatshops. President McKinley received Congressional authorization to invade Cuba and recognize the island's independence from Spain. May 29, 1898 some 17,000 American troops landed in Cuba. Lt. Col. Teddy Roosevelt led his troops up San Juan Hill to victory. Secretary of State, John Hay, proclaimed it a "splendid little war". In our 21st century, Cuba still remains a challenge for American diplomacy with Florida's politically powerful Cuban-American community protesting Castro's economic and political communist regime. Elian Gonzalez, a six-year-old, whose mother died during an attempt to reach Florida, became a "cause celebre" as distant Cuban American relatives fought with Elian's father for parental rights. Politicians, federal courts, law enforcement agencies and the Immigration service were entangled in the struggle between Cuban Americans and Cubans. New reporters vied with each other for photographs, instant 60-second analysis of events, and for increasing sales for their respective news outlets. News sensationalism prevailed.

At the turn of the 20th century, Theodore Roosevelt invoked the Sherman Anti-Trust Law of 1890 to break up oil and railroad monopolies while at the turn of the 21st century William Clinton's administration sought a break up of Microsoft, a huge computer software and Internet company. Then and now protests included sweatshop working conditions, child labor, governmental corruption and at-risk populations.

Unique to our time is an information age which brings new opportunities, but also new challenges. Cyberspace, nanotechnology, artificial intelligence, are paradigm shifts in theory and practice. Challenges include the threat that individuals can gain access to credit card information from slips thrown into garbage cans, from telephones, and from the Internet. There is potential to steal thousands of dollars through the illegal use of credit cards. On the global level, cryptography may be a threat to the world financial system.

The Internet can serve to improve our communication networks, to provide opportunities for individuals throughout the world, to access research information, and to encourage open dialogue. Nanotechnology, as Belsie (2000) points out, is opening up new frontiers for faster computers, medical robots, lighter spacecraft, with unimaginable inventions to come. On the other hand, Nanotechnology and the Internet can be a threat to comity, civility, and human decency. Belsie finds that some feel such fears are mere speculation while others call for slowing down and controlling the product of such research. We need to educate for cyber-civility as well to develop tolerance and acceptance for the rapidity of scientific discovery.

Showalter (1999) wrote about her experiences during the period she was president of the Modern Language Association. After publication of a book *Hystories*, that dealt with hysteria in modern culture she received angry e-mail messages referring to her as evil, fascist, a maggot, an ungrateful parasite, an imbecile, an antiquated hack trying to bolster a flagging career in academia, a homely loser, desperate, and an insulting e-mail, "If I had a dog with a mug like yours, I'd shave his behind and make him walk backwards". Showalter suggested that the potential for hostility, and anger is exacerbated by the one-way electronic communication and the mechanical impersonality of e-mail:

> ...Now more than ever, we need to learn to listen rather than to boycott, to consult rather than insult, and to search for common interests rather than to revel in divisive ideologies.
>
> *(Chronicle of Higher Education*: B5)

Anger and hostility are also inflamed by television and radio talk shows. Incivility, intolerance, hate language and indecency are found in America's workplaces from blue-collar workers through university faculty and administration. High on the list of challenges is the need for monitoring the media in all its forms. Selling the story regardless of accuracy, or spinning to make it interesting with attention-getting exaggeration, half-truths, and fabrication pose a threat to society. Television news magazines have been successfully sued for spreading lies that damaged corporate and individual reputations. Politicians often use the media to distort their opponents record, including outright lies. Public opinion polls often managed by media interests govern the nation's executive and legislative agendas. There are increased costs to run for office and organizations, individuals and lobbyists who have given large sums to politicians expect favorable legislation for their pet interests. The media is used by single special interest groups to repeat messages to effect the national debate on crucial issues. With media corporate mergers, fewer news organizations control much of the national news coverage.

Riechmann (1999) reported that a rising number of journalists, in addition to the public, view the media as lacking credibility. *The Pew Research Center for the People and the Press* interviewed 552 national and local journalists as well as news executives in print, television, radio, and the Internet on how they view themselves. The results suggest that journalists think reporting has become sloppier, that too many reporters use their articles and newscasts to speculate or state opinion. In addition, financial pressures hinder the quality of news coverage. When asked to cite chief problems facing journalists, over

50% of the respondents referred to sensationalism, a lack of objectivity and inaccurate reporting while some 40% cited too much emphasis on the bottom line, competition and declining audience and readership.

More journalists are seeking increased monitoring of the media to assure reliable dissemination of information essential in an open democratic society. James Fallows (1997) in his *Breaking News* suggested that media directors should spend less time on sportscaster-like analysis of how politicians were playing their game, should feel less compelled to flock to the spectacle of the moment in hopes of following the audience's fickle interest, should hold themselves responsible for the rise of public cynicism and should consider that the license they have to criticize and defame comes with an implied responsibility to serve the public. Sometimes CNN and public television provide a balance to sensationalism in newsmagazine programs but it too is often commercial. One-minute time slots providing superficial information without depth of analysis threaten the basis of a democratic society which depends for its existence on an informed public.

The age of technology brings ready access to information, and an expanded international consciousness, but also unrestricted pornography in homes, schools and offices through computer programs. Although there are cyberpatrols and other software programs to prevent youth access to pornography and other uncensored information. Sawyer (1999) reported on a preponderance of false and misleading information on the Internet which coupled with a declining ability to think critically, spells trouble in the future. In addition, Sawyer reported that the Internet leads to the creation of more barriers to person-to-person interaction.

Education will continue to be a lightning rod for social issues. Affirmative action, tenure, performance measurement, remedial education, sex education, educational standards, state department of education and legislative bureaucracy as well as standards for faculty evaluation will be heatedly debated into the distant future. Attacks on tenure and affirmative action at all educational levels will continue to expand unless there is a shift in political parties power base. Liberal versus conservative fringe groups will affect curriculum, standards, and value judgements out of proportion to their numbers in the general population. Both groups have learned how to use political networks to push ideological agendas. Parental lawsuits will make school administrators wary, and thus less inclined to develop innovative, creative, and outreach programs that my draw the ire of some single interest group. The search for tolerance, conflict resolution and consensus will continue in the future.

Educators tend to reinvent the wheel, unaware of our educational history. Efforts to improve educational achievement will be persistent and continuing. Nationwide emphasis on standardized test results to grade and rank schools and school districts have led to "teaching to the test" as well as overlooking important educational experiences that engage critical and independent thinking and analysis. In some cases, schools with a large number of exceptional at-risk children, teachers, administrators and parents know their school will be rated in the lowest category due to low student test results. Sporadic student, teacher, administrator and parent protests as well as some educators' questioning excessive reliance on standardized test results to measure student performance have not changed the philosophy of the assessment, testing and measurement bandwagon.

Historians of education will note however, that the multidimensional efforts to improve education through neighborhood schools, magnet schools, assessment and student testing, alternative evaluation systems, alternative school systems, have all been tried in the past with varying results. Educators thus tend to reinvent the wheel unaware of our educational history. Vouchers, charter schools, private and parochial schools, with notable exceptions, are attempts to avoid some of the problems faced by public schools that must take all students regardless of motivation, educational preparation, or adequate language skills.

At all levels of public education from elementary school through the university, teachers are finding a different student culture than in the past. Clayton (2000) described a changing student culture in higher education. He wrote of professors being confronted with undergraduate students who get up during lectures walking right in front of teachers. Students confront teachers with statements such as "This test is too hard, You shouldn't be asking us to do this stuff. You have to change it". Clayton continued by noting that early 21st century student culture involved widespread cheating, rudeness, disrespect, sleeping, eating, reading newspapers, foul language, spitting—examples of incivility in post-secondary classrooms. Although some believe the lack of discipline is a failure of instructors, others find a general pervasive culture of incivility that represents the larger society.

The challenge for teachers at all levels is to help students become acculturated to a learning culture. Post-secondary educators need to help undergraduate students adjust to a disciplined learning environment. Loco parentis (teachers stand in relation to students as does a parent with authority to maintain an environment conducive to learning) of colonial days may still be needed in our era. Teachers need to take on a parental role in helping young people mature. Professors need to shift from the old model of being a sage on the stage to being a sage on the side to maximize student involvement in learning. The new model includes being aware of students' ability to access knowledge and information more easily outside of traditional classrooms. The Internet, e-mail, distance learning are just a few of the competing educational delivery systems. Consumerism which stresses the primary goal of making the consumer satisfied has also infiltrated school philosophy. Students often expect to be entertained, given good grades and not excessively burdened with intellectual challenge. Whatever the situation, good students with strong parental support and guidance, will, in general, compete and achieve successfully at each educational level.

Golden (1999) finds new teaching models such as mastery learning have been implemented in Pentagon-run schools. Parent involvement through volunteering in schools has been helpful in maintaining student discipline, civility, decorum and academic achievement. Mastery learning is based on the belief that all children can learn, but at different rates, and has proven effective in Pentagon schools, especially for students-at-risk. Pentagon school officials work with parent volunteers and others to maintain a creative learning environment, effective discipline, and sensitivity to the constant movement of students to other military bases. In addition, extra time and effort is spent in intensive training of teachers. Fort Knox school officials use a variety of techniques for misbehavior including peer mediation, exile from regular classes, or in-school suspension. Commanding officers are called when student disruption cannot be controlled otherwise. Soldiers are told to keep their children in line or else face a dressing down or getting expelled from the base. This is another illustration of the implementation of loco parentis from the past.

In the future as in the past, public schools will seek to be all things to all people making real emphasis on a quality learning environment difficult. Conservative groups that support increased parental choice will expand alternative school options, although it appears not to have affected public school enrollment to date. The charter alternative school movement will continue to expand until more information is available about its degree of success. Schnaiberg (1998) reports on the research from California charter schools. Broad findings include:

- In most cases these schools are not yet held accountable for enhanced student achievement and are more likely to be held fiscally than educationally accountable, in part because districts are ambivalent about monitoring charters.
- Charter schools vary widely in the amount of operating autonomy they need or want from districts and in the demands they make on districts.
- Often charter schools must rely on private resources to supplement basic school aid, and their success in drawing corporate, foundation, or community aid is determined by the wealth of their communities and their leaders' connections.
- Charter schools have more control than most other public schools over which students are recruited and who can attend.
- Charter schools do their own recruiting and information dissemination, as well as setting out requirements for parental involvement and student performance or behavior.
- Attendance in charter schools is limited because the state does not pay for their students' transportation.

Charter school advocates noted that it is too early to make any definite statements about them since more than half of them are less than 2 years old. Charter school administrators and teachers continue make modifications to meet the challenges of operating an alternative school system and to respond to emerging parental and other litigation. Mainstream public schools have long faced increased student and parent litigation. President Clinton called for the establishment of 3,500 Charter Schools in 2000. One of the first Charter Schools was founded in 1992 in Minnesota. By mid-2000 there were 1,700 Charter Schools in the United States enrolling 250,000 students, still a fraction of the 53 million students in public schools. Kronholz (2000) noted that Charter Schools have implemented deregulation, pioneering technology, research and development, multiage classrooms, individualized student learning plans and teacher bonus programs in the years they have been operating, although educational history reveals a variety of such efforts in the past. In a period of entrepreneurship, expanding options and choices appeal to the population. In part, this accounts for the attempts to provide alternatives to the traditional school systems. Charter School founders are finding it increasingly difficulty to find funds to establish schools, often using old donated industrial, business, church buildings. Regardless of the obstacles the movement toward alternative school systems continues to grow both vouchers and Charter Schools.

Although the past, in retrospect, looks better than it really was, still it is clear to those of us who have been educators for several decades that school workplaces are less collegial and more adversarial than in the past. As in the larger society, confrontation, in-your-face argumentative communication, adversarial relationships and litigation has become a growing part of our lives in corporate and private sector institutions although there are periodic attempts to rediscover civility and comity.

The challenge of safety in our schools, workplaces and society continues to plague educators, parents, administrators, and the public. The Littleton, Colorado massacre where children killed children is one of the most well known in a series of school violence incidents. The problem of students seeking to imitate and top the violence of their peers plagues society. School officials in some schools have responded by installing surveillance equipment including metal detectors, school guards, police dogs, elimination of lockers and back-packs, and school uniforms. President Clinton called for a nationwide dialogue on school safety. Some schools are increasing the number of counselors, adding peace and aggression-control curriculum, providing school policy guidelines to encourage students to report violence-prone behavior of their peers, with confidentiality protections. Corporate and governmental efforts are underway to develop proactive strategies for employee behavior dysfunction. All such strategies cannot fully meet the challenge of random violence without family and community reporting initiatives. Individuals with a history of repeated violent behavior must be given continued counseling and supervision.

Meanwhile violence is seen in the movies, television, computer games, and everyday news reports of domestic and community conflicts. A casual perusal of a newspaper illustrates the point. Othon, Allen and Patrick (1999) reported that a 38-year-old mother who boarded a school bus near West Palm Beach, Florida to talk to kids who picked on her children, smashed the 52-year-old bus driver's kneecap, pulled out clumps of hair from her scalp and threw her glasses on the road. The incident occurred in front of 15 elementary school students. The bus driver spent several hours in the hospital and another driver took the children to school. Graham (1999) reported on a 15-year-old Tulsa high school sophomore, with no past problem record, who attempted to rape a 62-year-old high school teacher who had taught 26 years in the Tulsa public schools. The student attacked the teacher while she was getting supplies out of a closet, threw a cloth over her head, forced her to the floor while she screamed and fought him. Students and teachers nearby heard the commotion. One teacher opened the closet door and saw the youth naked from the waist down. Rumors at the school indicated it was part of a gang ritual. The teacher is taking an indefinite amount of time off. Such incidents reflect the increasing hostility and incivility in our society. State legislators are passing laws ranging from rules for courtesy to surveillance systems, and zero tolerance programs designed to increase school security and safety. Meanwhile lawsuits are proliferating against parents of children involved in school violence and against gun manufacturers.

An attempt to rediscover civility was the creation of the Penn Commission on *Society, Culture and Community*. The commission included a group of 48 prominent intellectuals, journalists, historians and sociologists who met twice a year to analyze a rising tide of meanness and incivility, that encourages violence, blocks social reform and disrupts reasoned national debate. Intolerance, provincialism, isolation, and anti-government hate groups all threaten national unity for the future. Another attempt to rediscover civility was a 100-member congressional retreat March 7-9, 1997, held in Hershey, Pennsylvania. Congress members and their families have been trying to hold an annual meeting since that date to explore ways of communicating with civility and decency (Van Patten, Stone and Chen 1997). Koch (1999) reported that a second three-day retreat ended with lawmakers hopeful of diminished venomous partisanship. The retreat included tours of the chocolate museum, trips to Gettysburg, a skating exhibition and line dancing lessons at a family country hoe-down. Nobel Laureate John Hume, who helped bring about a preliminary effort for a peace solution in Northern Island, gave the keynote address. With wives and children along for the retreat, civility held sway. Whether Congresspersons can continue avoiding emotional overtones of language resulting in legislative gridlock remains to be seen.

The Clinton impeachment proceedings, as well as persistent investigations of Department of Justice Janet Reno and other members of the Clinton administration, reflect the growing tendency toward litigation which affects all elements of the nation's social order. The proceedings also highlight and reflect a lawyer class increasingly powerful in the three branches of government. The composition of the political governing class in the United States although inching toward reflecting the nation's changing demographics, is still a male dominated governance system. Conservative versus liberal ideologies will continue to ebb and flow over the years ahead. With a record low in voter turnout for recent local, state and national elections, small numbers of unified vocal ideologues will wield power to control the national legislative agenda. Efforts to expand the voter turnout to include more of the working classes, the marginalized peoples (foreign born naturalized citizens), the nation's poor, those with few job skills and citizens at risk, will lead to a more representative legislative body. There is a growing tendency for single interest groups to take to the streets to influence politicians through protests. Over 100,000 Miami Cuban Americans waving Cuban flags closed streets, businesses, shops, and factories to express their feelings about Castro and United States Justice Department immigration policies. Other activists engage in training sessions learning how to shut down city traffic and business to protest for a wide variety of causes.

Diversity will continue to be a major theme throughout the 21st century. Corporate America increasingly relies on new immigrants, minorities and members of diverse cultures to provide human energy for the nation's service and industrial occupations. Organizations that require a large entry-level job pool, such as Tyson's chicken corporation, depend on culturally diverse populations to take jobs others in society do not want and will not seek. President William Clinton's appointments to the federal courts reflect a major effort to name more women and minorities as federal judges. Clinton has brought more diversity to federal courts than any other president in American history. His appointments since 1992 have doubled the number of women federal judges, increased the number of African-Americans on the bench by 56 percent and boosted the number of Hispanic judges by 39 percent, according to statistics collected by Alliance for Justice, a liberal Washington-based group that monitors judicial appointments (Richey, 1999). Richey continued by noting that if Clinton is not handicapped by extremists of the right and left in the next two years, there will be even more diverse population judges in the federal courts.

Meanwhile an economic boom, has led to increased employment of the nation's workforce. Although there are persistent pockets of poverty within the nation, progress is being made to address those issues through public and private initiatives. States, the federal government and corporations provide programs for needed upgrading of job skills. Major corporations, due to the economic boom, are importing foreigners to fill needed positions. Marriott and other corporations provide benefit and training programs for new hires from abroad.

Sixty-Six Years of Presidential Appointments to the Federal Bench	
President	Number of Judges
Franklin Roosevelt	197
Harry Truman	133
Dwight Eisenhower	177
John Kennedy	124
Lyndon Johnson	168
Richard Nixon	231
Gerald Ford	65
Jimmy Carter	262
Ronald Reagan	378
George Bush	189
Bill Clinton	301*
(November 99) Library of Congress 446	
*Source: Christian Science Monitor, Feb.17, 1999	

Askenas (1995) discussed a needed paradigm shift from structured to open systems with receptivity to emerging conditions as we move into our new century. Askenas suggested that it is necessary to eliminate those factors that are no longer applicable to a society and world in transition from a boundary thinking to a boundaryless organization. He recommended breaking boundaries between:

- Levels and ranks of people. Wal-Mart and Tyson are examples of corporations whose management insists on including all workers in open information systems through using the term "associates" for all employees as well as the wearing of common uniforms.

- Functions and disciplines. There must be freedom of communication among all parts of an organization. Isolation, excessive individualism are no longer appropriate to our current highly competitive marketplace when produce obsolescence is occurring more rapidly as witnessed in the computer industry. Horizontal teamwork, flexibility, and readiness to shift to jobs in growth areas are essential.
- Organizations, customers and suppliers. Organizations need to address market needs and be sensitive to shifts in customer concerns. No organization, no matter how large, how respected in the past, can afford to ignore marketplace trends in an age when product loyalty is nonexistent. These external factors increasingly affect organizations and lead to outsourcing of product production where necessary to maintain a competitive edge.
- A shift from size to speed, with computers smaller and more adaptable to rapid upgrade.
- Role clarity to flexibility. Workers in the future will need to be able to shift jobs, learn new skills and move rapidly to new locations as innovations require rethinking past functions and operations. Workers will need to function with role ambiguity due to the rapidity of market change.
- Specialization to integration. 21st Century workers will need to be ready, willing and able to integrate their functions with other sectors in corporate society.
- Control to integration for a positive future. Hierarchial arrangements necessary for routine requirements are no longer effective in an era of information cyber superhighways.

Workplaces will change as more generation Y (children born in the 1960s and 70s) enter the job market. These individuals will be more independent, less likely to accept authoritarian leadership, will question policy and decisions, and be more technologically oriented. Generation Y workers will not accept the life-long workplace loyalty of their parents. They have seen the disruptive results in their families of downsizing, restructuring, mergers, reorganization and machiavellian politics. Entrepreneurial generation Y workers will move from job to job to find employment satisfaction and be ready to start their own business, working out of homes. Their workplace world will have ceaseless change as new concepts become products of the future information age (Asinof, 1999). Younger generation Xers, are moving into the workforce with ever-more independence as well as new technical knowledge. Their ability to function well in the fast changing world of computer skills provides employers with lower cost hiring opportunities that may displace well qualified 30 and 40 year olds who have failed to keep up with the pace of change.

Every facet of life in our new century will be affected by the world-wide-web and the Internet. Investing, shopping, education, opinion polls, governmental decision-making, international trade and finance, research studies, and networking will be the wave of the future. Lenzner and Johnson interviewed Peter Drucker, (1997) and (1998). Drucker referred to multiple organizational structures, outsourcing, new educational delivery systems and the demise of traditional large universities to be replaced by off-campus satellites or two-way video. Carnevale (1999) reported on futurist Christopher J. Dede's prediction that distance education will be commonplace in higher education and that in his lifetime refusal by a faculty member to use distance education will be considered professional malpractice. Shaking up traditional university delivery systems, Kaplan Educational Centers opened in the fall of 1998 the first Internet law degree program at Concord University. U.S. Supreme Court Justice Ruth Bader Ginsburg, and others reacted by noting that Concord University School of Law is an institution that relies too heavily on technology and consequently loses the shared enterprise of legal education. In response Concord's Dean Goetz, said communication with professors is enhanced through e-mail, telephone and on-line discussions (Mangan, 1999).

Challenges to traditional university delivery systems will increase in our new century. Already Harvard University wants to rein in one of its star professors from offering videotaped lectures to Concord law students. Professor Arthur Miller was asked to terminate his contract with Concord, and Harvard added a new rule requiring professors to get permission from their Dean and the corporation that governs the university prior to serving as a teacher, researcher or consultant to any Internet-based university (Marcus, 1999). The Internet challenge to traditional enterprises will change the landscape of our future. The possibilities of the Internet Age have barely been tapped and paradigm shifts will continue.

Coates (1996,1997) found that there will be an increase in women executives, who will push for flexible work schedules as a well as a new corporate culture. Coates, a Futurist Consultant, stressed the trend toward more attention to quality-of-life cycle including child and elderly care. Both Coates and Askenas report on global networking for increased world markets that will be used to improve quality and exports.

A message for the future generations was given by Rushworth M. Kidder in his 1987 book *Agenda For the Future*. Kidder interviewed twenty-two leading thinkers in the world asking each of them to respond to the question "what are the major issues mankind will face in the 21st century?". Although there were many responses, a common theme involved the importance of trust, compassion, dignity, and a search for common values of consensus. The importance of improving our local communities with personal involvement was found to be an essential building block to a more humane future for the world's peoples. Kidder (1996) also found a universal value system of love, truthfulness, fairness, freedom, unity, tolerance, responsibility and respect for human life. These are the values that will provide a civilized, humane future for everyone. The search for comity, civility, and tolerance for others will continue. Demographics within the United States require educators, businesses, industrialists, governmental officials, local, state and federal courts in their deliberations to stress the necessity of honoring, treasuring, and respecting diversity of ethnicity, culture, age, gender, race and lifestyle preferences. Multiculturalism is the open door to the future of our pluralistic social democratic experiment. It is a future that can enrich, enliven our citizens and provide a mosaic of patterns, forms, combinations of languages, meanings, folkways and mores that ought ideally to reflect America's seamless efforts to expand economic and social justice for its peoples. A new language of appreciation for our diversity and its rich promise of "the best is yet to come" will unleash boundless energy for a better tomorrow. The trends and issues explored in this book represent a new language for a new era with the expectation that the lag between exponential technological change and the individual ability to cope with it will decrease until our information age becomes a universally accepted tool for the advancement of civilization.

References

Asinof, Lynn (1999, November 29). "Go With the Flows". *The Wall Street Journal*: R6.

Askenas, et. Al. (1995). *The Boundaryless Organization*. San Francisco; Jossey-Bass.

Belsie, Laurent (2000, April 13). "Nanotechnology's Descent into Matter's Minuteness". *The Christian Science Monitor*: 20, 21.

Carnevale, Dan (1999, October 22). "Distance Education Can Bolster the Bottom Line, A Professor Argues". *The Chronicle of Higher Education*: A 60.

Clayton, Mark (2000, March 21). "Professors Struggle to Route Out Rudeness". *The Christian Science Monitor*: 16.

Coates, Joseph F (1997, December 18). *Transforming Issues for the Future*. Personal Communication with the Author, Washington, D.C.

Coates, Joseph F. (1996). " Scientific Breakthrough". *Encyclopedia For the Future*. New York: MacMillan: 822-825.

Drucker, Peter F. (1998, October 5). "Management's New Paradigms". *Forbes*: 152-176.

Fallows, James (1997). *Breaking the News: How the Media Undermine American Democracy*. New York: Vintage Books Division of Random House: 268-270.

Golden, Daniel (1999, December 22). "Making the Grade: Pentagon-Run Schools Excel in Academics, Defying Demographics".*The Wall Street Journal*: A1, A6.

Kidder, Rushworth M. (1987). *An Agenda For the 21st Century*. Cambridge, Massachusetts: The M.I.T. Press: 204-205.

Kidder, Rushworth M. (1994, August, July). "Universal Human Value: Finding an Ethical Common Ground". *The Futurist*: 8-13.

Kidder, Rushworth M. (1995, September, October). "Tough Choices: Why It's Getting Harder to Be Ethical". 29-32.

Koch, Wendy (1999, March 22). "People Were Crying' At Second Retreat for Lawmakers". *USA Today*: 11 A.

Kronholz, June (2000, April 11). "Defying Convention, Superintendent Takes a Chance On Charters". *The Wall Street Journal:* A 1, A 10.

Lenzner, Robert and Johnson, Stephen S. (1997, March 10). "Seeing Things as They Really Are." *Forbes*: 127.

Mangan, Katherine (1999, September 24). "Justice Ginsburg Questions Internet-Only Law School". *The Chronicle of Higher Education*: A 36.

Marcus, Amy Dockser (1999, November 22). "Seeing Crimson: Why Harvard Law Wants To Rein in One of Its Star Professors". *The Wall Street Journal*: 1, 10.

Othon, Nancy L., Allen, C. Ron, and Patrick, Kelly (1999, May 19). "Woman Charged in Assault on Driver". *Sun-Sentinel*: Section B, 1.

Richey, Warren (1999, February 17). "Clinton Remaking Reagan Bench". *The Christian Science Monitor*: 1, 5.

Richey, Warren (1999, March 24). "When Cops Bust In, News Crews in Tow". *The Christian Science Monitor:* 1, 4.

Riechmann, Deb (1999, March 31). "The Media Aren't Believable, Many U.S. Journalists Concede". *Tulsa World:* C 8.

Sawyer, Deborah (1999, February). "The Pied Piper Goes Electronic". *The Futurist*: 42-46.

Schnaiberg, Lynn (1998, December 9). "Report: California Charters Fall Short on Promises". *Education Week*: 8.

Showalter, Elaine (1999, January 15). "Taming the Rampant Incivility in Academe". *The Chronicle of Higher Education*: B 4. B 5.

Van Patten, James, Stone, George C. and Chen, Ge (1997). *Individual and Collective Contributions to Humaneness in Our Time*: vi, vii.

Definitions

Artificial Intelligence. Use of computers in a virtual environment to formulate decisions based on ability to retrieve information from a variety of sources. Difficult to determine accuracy or inaccuracy of information on which decisions are based.

American Enterprise Institute. A conservative think tank analyzing longer term trends for business and industry.

Cyberspace. Information available from the Internet without the use of traditional libraries and or other sources from specific locations.

Cryptology. Information in code to maintain transactions in privacy. The art of encryptology.

Environmental Scanning. Analysis of the mores and folkways of the culture to determine best options for alternative scenarios for the future. Focus is on long term trends of outside influences on public and private institutions.

Genetic Engineering. Use of latest medical research to modify genes in pursuit of eliminating disease and enhancing the quality of life.

Hudson Institute. Major think tank for predicting and prophesizing future trends and directions. Positive approach to challenges facing social institutions with faith in knowledge available and in development to solve problems.

Internet. Access to information from cyberspace. Massive amounts of information available from a variety of sources with rapid access.

Paradigm. Belief systems based on previous data and information.

Rand Corporation. Liberal think tank for analyzing trends and issues. Using researchers for short periods of time to analyze timely topics.

Strategic Planning. Future forecasting designed to prepare for unexpected events. Continency planning employing feedback loops.

Synergy. Multidimensional influences with a totality greater than the sum of its part. Purposeful change for effective production. Often refers to crisis planning.

System Breaks. Unexpected events, happenings, occurrences requiring alternative scenarios to provide for redirection and restructuring of leadership and organizational systems. Engages feedback loops to prepare for contingencies.

World Future Society. Founded by Edward Cornish to provide an outlet to disseminate innovations and positive change forces occurring throughout the world. Edward Cornish was formerly a reporter for the *National Geographic Magazine* who found exciting new developments to improve the quality of life throughout the world. He saw a need to make this information available for others to make positive economic, social, political changes and founded the World Future Society to meet this need.

Y2K. Modifying computers in order to deal with the change to 2000 for the 1900s.

Index

References are to page numbers. Definition of terms are not included, they are shown on page 215.